: can.

**Clark Public Library**

**Clark, N. J.**

**388-5999**

# HEAR THE WIND BLOW!

# HEAR THE WIND BLOW!

## Poems of Protest & Prophecy

By

## JOHN BEECHER

*With an introduction by Maxwell Geismar*

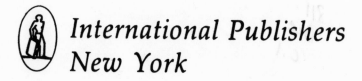

*International Publishers*
*New York*

For Barbara. *"Two shall become one."*

ACKNOWLEDGMENTS

I wish to express my gratitude to James S.
Allen and Walter Lowenfels for their help in
assembling the poems in this volume. Nearly
all are taken from earlier books of mine, HERE
I STAND (1941), ALL BRAVE SAILORS (1945),
LAND OF THE FREE (1956), IN EGYPT LAND
(1960), REPORT TO THE STOCKHOLDERS
(1962), and TO LIVE AND DIE IN DIXIE (1966).
Prior to book publication most had appeared
in various journals both here and abroad: *At-
tack* (Tokyo), *Brand X, Coastlines, Commonweal,
Continuum, Fellowship, Folio, Impetus, Liter-
ary Art Press, Literaturnaya Gazeta* (Moscow),
*Mainstream, The Minority of One, Monthly Re-
view, Morning Star Quartos, National Guardian,
Nea Hestia* (Athens), *Negro Digest, New Masses,
New York Post, The New Republic, New York
Times, Omnibus, Poems & Pictures, renaissance,
Rights, Siempre!* (Mexico City), *Social Digest,
Tachydromos Egyptos* (Alexandria), *The Texas
Quarterly, Twice A Year, Way* and *The Western
Poet.*
A number of the poems herein were first
brought together in UNDESIRABLES, a pam-
phlet of my work edited by James Singer for
the New Poets series of his Goosetree Press.
My thanks to the publications listed.
My thanks also to Sanda Aronson for the wood
block used as the frontispiece and to my wife,
Barbara, for the book design.
J.B.

# Introduction

By MAXWELL GEISMAR

It is ironical but in a sense logical that an authentic "proletarian" poet today—one who writes directly from the experience of the people, from the depths of poor people's lives, and mainly poor black people; a poet who speaks their language, and whose poetry in turn can be understood by these people—should be the descendant of a famous old New England family of dissenters, iconoclasts, atheists and freethinkers (among the clergymen members), ardent abolitionists, native non-conformists.

It is ironical, logical, and yet perhaps unexpected and doubly refreshing that John Beecher should fill all these requirements as a rebellious talent bringing to modern times the spirit of his famous ancestors. I might also add he is a very fine poet who speaks directly to my soul (and to yours, I am sure) after a long period when poetry was no longer trying to speak to anybody except the poetic elite—or shall we say clique? In Robert McAlmon's fine book on the 1920s, *Being Geniuses Together*, just lately revived along with Kay Boyle's Memoirs, he speaks of T.S. Eliot not altogether reverently. "I decided to get in touch with T. S. Eliot," he wrote, "although his cautious articles on criticism did not impress me, nor did his erudition, scholarship, or his lack of a sense of either life or literature. His moldy poetry struck me as the perfect expression of a clerkly and liverish man's apprehension of life, and to me he was Prufrock."

It is Eliot's spirit, however, which has dominated modern poetry down to the elegaic, self-centered, and to me rather weary "confessions" of Robert Lowell. John Beecher's poetry, so much to the contrary, so proud, angry, rebellious; so full of moral dignity and so rocklike—and, believe me, written out of an equal but radical erudition and scholarship—has been one of the very few dissenting voices during this period. Most of the books from which this volume of collected poems has been made were either printed privately or by small radical presses and magazines. It was only indeed in the early '60s, when the oppressive and intimidating atmosphere of the Cold War period had lifted, more than momentarily, as we hope, and the lethargic spell over the national consciousness had been broken by the civil-rights campaign in the South, white and black a-like, that Beecher's poetry suddenly came into prominence.

I frankly don't know, nor too much care, how John Beecher gets his marvelous effects in those poetic lines which are carved out from the common speech of the people, or from the beautiful black southern dialects. There are, on the other hand, very subtle, complex, almost metaphysical poems in this collection where Beecher shows what he can do when he wants to work with a more "literary," or perhaps just a more Latinic and poly-syllabic mode of language. To achieve the limpid, lucid simplicity of most of these poems, in a poetic style that, even with some Whitmanesque references, is completely *fresh* and original, an artist must obviously know how to handle the most difficult modes of prosody—must have spent his lifetime, as I suspect John Beecher has, in perfecting the exact kind of "simplicity" he wants to achieve. What he does is to give to the various dialects of our country, south, midwest, west and north, a kind of added height and dignity, while preserving all of the folk knowledge, humor and earthiness. What he does is to embed these folk tongues into the matrix of our literature.

We get in these poems also a kind of informal yet permanent chronicle of the "American century," from the depression years in the steel towns and southern farms to the epoch of Black Power and Vietnam. And what makes this national chronicle so rare is simply that it is viewed constantly, as in the opening verse of Thoreau, "Homage to a Subversive," from the *underside* of things, the radical and ironically "subversive" side, the side that has been so consistently blocked out and covered over during these years. We have had a plethora of Cold War accounts which have distorted the whole meaning of our national history from the Civil War to our "containment" of Russia and our even more fatal "containment" of China; from John Brown, who was suddenly declared "insane" in the modern period, to the "mad and aggressive" Chairman Mao who has not yet invaded a single foreign country. It is not history we lack in our period, but the courage of men like John Beecher to see history whole, and to record it so beautifully in these verse chronicles and narratives.

7

In any event, another point of these poems is that they *are* narrative in essence and contain dramatic movement. Most of the longer ones are based on historical episodes as recreated in Beecher's vision of them; the shorter ones contain the essence of a man or woman's being, often in ten lines, the essence of a human life, or a place, or an event. What a relief—after decades of cryptic, convoluted modern verse about remote and obscure states of human subjectivity, and "alienation." One might say again that nothing human is alien to John Beecher, and what he sees is not at all a mysterious contemporary disease (such as the death of God), but a corrupt social system that all too often not merely alienates its second-class citizens, as based on wealth and skin color, but destroys them, and not merely theoretically but *actually* through the process of armed violence.

Thus the poetry in this volume starts with the industrial conflict of the 1930s in the southern steel towns: what violence, but what hope in that perhaps last peak of our society! (This whole vision of the South which Beecher conveys is an antidote to both Faulkner's later romanticism—and race reversion—and to Richard Wright's magnificent black nightmares.) There is the poem called "The Odyssey of Thomas Benjamin Harrison Higgenbottom," which conveys in brief, but how eloquently, the whole story of the small farmer's obliteration on the national scene.

There is (to mention only a very few highlights of a book which is altogether comprised of good poetry) the epical verse, "In Egypt Land." This is the story of the first farmers' union, organized by the blacks who had nothing more to lose, joined by the whites, and its bloody extermination by the "laws,"—told here with so much compassion and human feeling, dramatic power and lyrical grief, as to make you feel you have *participated* in the tragedy which is so classical and yet so homespun. "Here I Stand," written in the 1940s is another poem of both classical and epic stature that, though an intensely personal chronicle, is one of the best accounts of the darkening Cold War atmosphere, so oppressive and so fatal to all creative thought and work—an officially created cultural climate that still haunts us, that distorts all our historical perspective even through the '60s, and has run the United States off the

8

time-track of contemporary society. That is the reason we are always so wrong, and so dangerous in our foreign policy, working always from one disaster to another; and I see no remedy for this until our surviving Cold War figures, politicians, educators, journalists, artists, die off or are put away in the national interest.

There is indeed a whole chorus of poems here which describe and record the effects of "the air that kills." Perhaps I value this poetry so much just because I came to the same conclusions *before* I had read John Beecher's verse; namely, that the whole literary establishment in the 1940s and '50s was a complete fraud, working, whether consciously or not, whether paid-off or voluntarily, to further the interests of the "Free World" and a now-discredited American foreign policy.

Now I have only just begun to describe this book of John Beecher's poems; I would only add that Beecher's sense of the contemporary scene is so unique just because he understands the whole revolutionary core of the American past. In appearance and posture, as well as in his poetry, John Beecher reminds me of nothing so much as the Last of the Abolitionists. This collection of his poetry is so good that I feel honored and privileged to pay homage to it.

*Harrison, New York*
*June 1968*

# CONTENTS

# III
## 1941-1944
## THEIR BLOOD CRIES OUT

# IV
## 1955-1959
## AN AIR THAT KILLS

# V
## 1961-1965
## WOKE UP THIS MORNING

# Prologue

HOMAGE TO A SUBVERSIVE
*For H. D. T. 1817-1862*

Soon, Henry David, wind will fill the land
saluting your centenary. Do you
suppose that alma mater's orators
at her memorial solemnities
will quote: "What branches of learning did you
find offered while at Harvard, Mr. Thoreau?"
"All of the branches and none of the roots."
And will Concord's divines in eulogies
of you dwell on the public scandal of
your unchurched life and unrepentant end?
"It's time to make your peace with God, Henry!"
"I'm not aware," the long-faced death-watch heard
you quip, "that God and I have ever quarreled."

The pietists who con your works by rote
forswear you and themselves with servile oaths
to placate golfing clerics, bawds of the press,
snoopers, war-hawks, kept Congressmen. Silent
they stand while lying leaders make our name
odious to men, shield tyrants with our might,
huckster new-packaged servitude for freedom,
and dub the peoples' butchers "democrats".
The coffle of pampered house-slaves will dare hymn
you dead. Come back! They'll turn you in. "How should
a man behave toward this government
today? I answer, that he cannot without
disgrace associate himself with it."

13

# I
## *1932-1940*

### WHOSE AMERICA?

# REPORT TO THE STOCKHOLDERS

### I

he fell off his crane
and his head hit the steel floor and broke like an egg
he lived a couple of hours with his brains bubbling out
and then he died
and the safety clerk made out a report saying
it was carelessness
and the craneman should have known better
from twenty years experience
than not to watch his step
and slip in some grease on top of his crane
and then the safety clerk told the superintendent
he'd ought to fix that guardrail

### II

out at the open hearth
they all went to see the picture
called *Men of Steel*
about a third-helper who
worked up to the top
and married the president's daughter
and they liked the picture
because it was different

### III

a ladle burned through
and he got a shoeful of steel
so they took up a collection through the mill
and some gave two bits
and some gave four
because there's no telling when

IV

the stopper-maker
puts a sleeve brick on an iron rod
and then a dab of mortar
and then another sleeve brick
and another dab of mortar
and when he has put fourteen sleeve bricks on
and fourteen dabs of mortar
and fitted on the head
he picks up another rod
and makes another stopper


V

a hot metal car ran over the Negro switchman's leg
and nobody expected to see him around here again
except maybe on the street with a tin cup
but the superintendent saw what an ad
the Negro would make with his peg leg
so he hung a sandwich on him
with safety slogans
and he told the Negro just to keep walking
all day up and down the plant
and be an example


VI

he didn't understand why he was laid off
when he'd been doing his work
on the pouring tables OK
and when men with less age than he had
weren't laid off
and he wanted to know why
but the superintendent told him to get the hell out
so he swung on the superintendent's jaw
and the cops came and took him away

VII

he's been working around here ever since there was
    a plant
he started off carrying tests when he was fourteen
and then he third-helped
and then he second-helped
and then he first-helped
and when he got to be sixty years old
and was almost blind from looking into furnaces
the bosses let him
carry tests again

VIII

he shouldn't have loaded and wheeled
a thousand pounds of manganese
before the cut in his belly was healed
but he had to pay his hospital bill
and he had to eat
he thought he had to eat
but he found out
he was wrong

IX

in the company quarters
you've got a steelplant in your backyard
very convenient
gongs bells whistles mudguns steamhammers and slag-
    pots blowing up
you get so you sleep through it
but when the plant shuts down
you can't sleep for the quiet

*19  Whose America?*

## FIRE BY NIGHT

when the burnt black bodies of the homeless
were found in the embers of the Negro church
into which they had crept to sleep on the floor
the wails of the people traveled down the cold wind
and reached the ears of the rich on the mountain
like the distant whistle of a fast train coming


## OLD MAN JOHN THE MELTER

old man John the melter
wouldn't tap steel till it was right
and he let the superintendents rave
he didn't give a damn about tonnage
but he did give a damn about steel
so they put him on the street
but he had plenty of money
and he drove up and down in his "Wily Knecht"
a floatin pallus he called it
with a Pittsburg stogie in his whiskers
and played poker at the Elks club
and the steel got sorrier and sorrier
and rails got to breaking under trains
and the railroads quit buying
and the mill shut down
and then the superintendents asked old man John
to come and tell them what was wrong with the steel
and he told them
too many superintendents

## ENSLEY, ALABAMA: 1932

The mills are down.
The hundred stacks
are shorn of their drifting fume.
The idle tracks
rust. . .
Smeared red with the dust
of millions of tons of smelted ore
the furnaces loom —
towering, desolate tubes —
smokeless and stark in the sun. . .
Powerhouse cubes
turbines hummed in,
platesteel mains the airblast thrummed in
are quiet, and the sudden roar
of blown-off steam. . .
At night
the needle gleam
where the ladle poured at the pig machine,
the deep smoulder of an iron run
and the spreading light
of molten slag over the sleeping town
are seen
no more
now mills and men are down.

# RUN OF THE MINE

### I

I went into tight places for them (he said)
when the inspector had condemned a gallery
I went in and I got men to go with me
and we dug coal and kept our mouths shut
and I thought when the time came I needed it
they would go into a tight place for me
but because I had a foaming fit on the job
from high blood pressure and because I was old
and they thought I might cost them money
if I died at work in the mine
they fired me and put *unsatisfactory*
on my discharge slip and when I wanted to know
what unsatisfactory thing I had done
they said to come back next week for a statement

### II

he went to work in Pennsylvania
up north where he could earn more mining
and every month for three years he sent money home
to keep up the payments on the house and furniture
and when he couldn't stay away from his wife
and children in the south any longer
he came home to his old job at Camp Seven
that year it rained and rained and then rained
and though his house like all the other houses there
was perched on stilts to escape the regular floods
the water came in and kept on rising
and when it went down the cheap veneer
of the just paid for furniture peeled off
and the floor of the nearly paid for house
buckled and the walls leaned and the roof caved

### III

one side of his old face is black and smooth
but the other looks as if the flesh had been poured
molten on the bones and had cooled like slag
lustrous bluepocked and with crater cups
like a photograph of the surface of the moon
and the eye is absent and even the eyebrow

### IV

at Lewisburg there is coal in the ground
not inexhaustible yet unexhausted
and on top there is coal on the spur tracks
gondolas heaped with it tons upon tons
a share of which was mined by Ben P Jones
who may be seen any day on the slate dump
accompanied by his family of five
winnowing the refuse for nuggets of coal
lest they freeze through the winter approaching

### V

the Sayreton miners complained and they said
what with the payrate slashed nearly in half
and what with making just two shifts a week
not much was left after stoppage came out
stoppage for rent on the houses they lived in
for medical care of their families
and a doctor when their women gave birth
the Sayreton bosses replied that the stoppage
was optional. . . a roof over your head
was optional and medicine for your children
optional. . . optional to have a doctor
at the birthing time. . . all this was optional

# GOOD SAMARITAN

The Negro walked his shoes out looking for work
and when there was nothing left to eat in his house
he deferentially asked for food
and the charitable city after due
investigation which revealed that he really
had a wife and four children and wasn't just
lying allotted them a sack of flour
and half a pound of salt pork and other
plain substantial foods to be consumed
at the rate of nine cents worth daily per each
adult and four and a half cents worth per child
if the ration was to last the week. . .
or they could if they preferred eat well
two days and go hungry five. . . that was up to them. . .

Now the city out of its profound acquaintance
with Negro nature knew that it wasn't sufficient
simply to feed an idle black however badly
in order to keep him in his proper place
but that his mind should be kept occupied
or rather kept unoccupied by thoughts
disturbing to his happy loyal nature. . . nor
should he be allowed to get the idea
that he could eat without working lest he
be spoiled for good. . . in order therefore
that he might the better digest the bread
of charity and feel that he had in a way
earned it he was ordered to work two days
a week on the roads in exchange for food
worth considerably less than one day's labor. . .
On those days he trudged with other of the city's
beneficiaries five miles out to swing

pick and shovel nine hours in red mud and tough
chert rock and then trudged in again to town. . .
sometimes they were lucky enough to ride in
on the back of a truck with a Negro driver
(they never had the impudence to hail a white)
and rest their blisters and run up less
of a hunger. . . every mile saved was a biscuit
earned. . .

        One hot evening as they were tramping
homewards in their rag-swathed wrecks of shoes
while the white folks' cars went whiffing by
pneumatic and easeful and lulling with waft
of wind in passing within a foot at fifty
a ramshackle truck came by headed toward town
with a Negro at the wheel. . . they yelled. . . the truck
swerved slowing on the shoulder. . . they cut across
the road to jump it. . . he last. . . clenching
his teeth as he ran on swollen bloody feet. . .
LOOK OUT they screamed. . . and a fast car hit him

The shattered bundle was picked up from the road
by the other Negroes and stowed in a car
driven by a good white man who had stopped
after the accident to see if he could help
and offered to take him to the hospital
since his car was so much faster than the truck
He sped wide-open into town while his burden
fouled the back-seat cushions with clotting pool
and reek of puke. . . and five minutes later
deposited the Negro unconscious but breathing
in the arms of science at the charity hospital
to furnish some interne a bit of practice. . .
It takes a lot to kill one of the sons
of bitches said the interne on the receiving ward

25  *Whose America?*

waggling the fractured limbs of the Negro
to see if the pain would make him come to
and since it didn't deciding not to waste
any anaesthetic on the black bastard. . .

The good white man who had brought the patient in
told the hospital authorities
that the Negro had been struck by a southbound car
with a Florida license. . . woman driving. . .
hadn't stopped. . . hit and run. . . damned outrage. . .
when the car hit the poor nigger it threw
him high in the air. . . lit square on his head. . .
yes he'd tried to get the number. . . was a 3
a 6 and a 4 in it. . . couldn't get it for sure. . .
woman must have been clocking around seventy. . .
If he'd been able to get that number
he sure would turn it in on her because
he believed niggers ought to get a square deal
and he wasn't a man to cover anything up
even if it was a white woman in the wrong. . .
no couldn't say what kind of a car it was
you couldn't tell cars apart any more
might have been a Buick or an Olds. . .
Would he give his name? Well if they'd just as soon
he'd rather not. . . he'd done what he could for
the poor nigger stopping and bringing him in
and messing his car all up. . . and if he gave his name
there was no telling what it'd lead to. . .
some jackleg lawyer might take up the case
and haul him into court and waste his time
but he would call up in a couple of days
and find out if the authorities located
that Florida car. . . and if they did he would
be glad to testify and see that the poor

nigger got justice whatever it cost. . .
and then the good white man left in a hurry. . .

Right after he left the Negro's friends
arrived in the slow truck and hung around
afraid to ask anything but wanting to know
if he was surely dead before they told his wife
and finally one of them sidled up to the window
and asked and the girl said he'd been taken
to the operating room and then she asked
had any one of them got that Florida
license number and they said they didn't
know nothin about no Florida license number
and she said hadn't a Florida car hit him
and they said the white gentleman what hit him
done carried him to the hospital in his car

## THE SPECTRE IN PLAIN DAY

The chancred denizens of these foul haunts
Lean out of broken windows and entice
Your boys with frowsy blandishments, thirsty
To drink up their innocence, for men are wise
And sate their appetites on cleanlier flesh,
At least when they are sober. But this goes on
With profit to someone, and will go on,
One knows, while the high stars hold their courses
And the high sheriff winks in the court-house
And the spectre in plain day walks unchallenged
      amongst us.

## VULCAN AND MARS OVER BIRMINGHAM

Here
banal upon his parapet
the god of work gesticulates aloft
clumsily moulded from ore
of the marvelous mountain. The vermilion cleft
of the highway beneath is not
banal though, exposing the iron-fraught strata.

Blurred
by distance and the haze
of many thousand smokes
the city—born of this mountain—lies
gangling over its ridges and valleys, a tired
child-city, full of aches
and growing pains, unsure of its powerful nature.

Stranger,
down there will yet
spread a city adult, no soft
leechlike urban creature
but essential unto its day. What will be left
after the old antagonist wings overhead is not
revealed though, locked in the iron-fraught future.

## APPALACHIAN LANDSCAPE

Sick and scrawny lies the land, denuded
Of forest, sapped of fertility,
Gutted of coal, the integument of life
Flayed utterly from it and bleeding
Its last weak pulse away down washes and gullies.

Scrawny and sick on the stoops of their shacks,
Idle, dejected are the folk of this land.
One sometimes observes them crawling
About their irremediable fields or plodding
Unwashed homewards from their failing mines.


## JEFFERSON DAVIS INAUGURAL
*Capitol Portico: Montgomery, Alabama*

A brazen star
marks where his haughty feet were set
who later fled
in womanly disguise while near and far
the vengeful victor spoke in flame
and insult till the broken land was red
not with blood and embers only but with shame

A star inlaid
marks where he postured on the marble for a day
with his people ranged below
and seeking to stay history he bayed
the sun like Joshua
The sun impenitently set
and once more rose on irreversible woe

29   *Whose America?*

## NEWS ITEM

I see in the paper this morning
where a guy in Gadsden Alabama
by the name of John House
who was organizing rubber workers in a lawful union
against the wishes of the Goodyear Rubber Company
          and the Sheriff of Etowah County
was given a blood transfusion
after being beaten with blackjacks
by five parties unknown.
The Police Chief is "investigating"
and I have a pretty good idea of what that will amount to.
A few years ago they took Sherman Dalrymple
President of the United Rubber Workers of America
out of a peaceable union meeting in Gadsden
and right in front of the Etowah County court house
before the eyes of hundreds including the Sheriff
the deputies
beat him almost to death.
Plenty more
who have tried to organize workers in Etowah County
have had the same thing happen to them.

The Government of the United States
should know about John House
but maybe they won't notice the little item
on the back pages of the Birmingham paper
because the front pages are all filled up with Hitler
and how he is threatening democracy
so I am asking
the Government of the United States
to pay a little attention to this.
To defend democracy

the Government of the United States
is building a lot of munitions plants around the country
with the people's money
because the people want democracy defended
One of these plants is being built at Gadsden
in Etowah County Alabama-
twenty four million dollars worth of plant to be exact-
twenty four million dollars of the people's money
going into a county
which isn't even a part of the United States
Or is it?


I think it would be a good idea
for the Government of the United States
to look into this
and see if they can't persuade Etowah
to come back in the Union
If persuasion won't work they might try a little coercion
because the laws of the United States ought to be made
    good
and as luck would have it
there's a great big army camp at Anniston
just thirty miles away
Not long ago I drove through this camp
and I saw new barracks and tents all over the scenery
and thousands upon thousands of soldiers
getting ready to defend democracy
They looked to me
as if they could do it
and they looked to me
as if they wanted a try at it
Maybe they could get a little practice over in Etowah
before they pitch into
the foreign fascists

31   *Whose America?*

# THE FACE YOU HAVE SEEN

April has come
April of 1941
the month we were waiting for
through the dark winter
begins. . .

The old man with the face you have seen
tough and kind and none too bright
but lasting
the face you have seen getting on the streetcar
at the mill gate stop
or the gusty corner
now under the blood-soaked handkerchief
looks out at you
with blood oozing down the forehead
from under the handkerchief
and blood on the collar of the old overcoat. . .

"We'll be in it by April"
they said.
Sure enough
the fighting has started
and this old man with the face you have seen
is the first to get hurt.

"Whose America?" somebody asked
and is this the answer?
Another old man
with a face you also have seen
a face you have seen getting out of limousines
at the bank entrance
or the War Department

asks us to remember '94
when the army broke the Pullman strike.
That was a time to forget
I thought
and I think
right now is the worst of all possible times
to ask us to remember. . .

It is April now
the month we were waiting for
but was it for this
that we waited-
the berserk cop with the brandished club
the armored bus spraying gas on the pickets
the mobbing howl of the press
and the rabies in Congress-
"to the electric chair with the strikers"?

Whose America anyhow?
Now in this April
we need to find out.
Yes, all of us need to know whose America
because if it really isn't the America of the old man
with the face which is our face
tough and kind and none too bright
but lasting-
then, well
we are going to have to do some thinking
some mighty hard thinking. . .

This is the April we were waiting for.
This is the April.
This April.
Now.


33   *Whose America?*

## BEAUFORT TIDES

Low tide.
The scavenging gulls
scour the reaches of mud.
No slavers ride
at anchor in the roads. Rotting hulls
are drawn up on the shore.

Full stood
the tide here
when through this colonnaded door
into the raw land passed bond and free,
the one in hope leading the other in fear,
chained each to each by destiny.

Not only tide
but time and blood
can turn, can ebb and flow.
Time ebbs, blood flows, the fear
shows in the master's eye while jubilee
bursts from the bondsman's throat.

Now
no shout
rings out.
Neither hopes. Both fear.
What future tide will free
these captives of their history?

## THE ODYSSEY OF THOMAS BENJAMIN HARRISON
### HIGGENBOTTOM

Way back when I was young the land was new.
I taken the habit of cleaning it up
for people. Leased me a farm from an Indian
when I got married. We made out all right.
We couldn't complain. Of course we taken fever
and chills. Next farm we rented over by Slick,
but they struck oil on it and put us off.
Good river bottom land I farmed on next,
belonging to a banker. I cleaned it up
and then we moved to Kansas. My wife's folks
lived there. Some wheat growers come in and fenced
the open range. We sold our stock and moved
on back to Oklahoma, figuring
we might do better in country that we knew.
We found a place close to Muskogee
and made a bumper crop, the best there was
in all that neighborhood, then moved again
to Tahlequah and stayed two years. Found me
a bigger farm and bought it from the bank.
Most of that country then was open range.
Got me a bunch of high-class cattle. That
is where the drought first caught us. If I
could just look forward like I do backwards!
To quiet the mortgage on my stock I sold
some cattle off, ten dollars for each cow
I'd paid a hundred for. I owed the bank
a little land note so I sold two hounds,
two running hounds, for a hundred sixty-five.
Two hounds brought more than sixteen head of cattle!
We stayed five years before we sold that farm
and bought a larger one. We made the best

and biggest corn and cotton crop in all
that country our first year but when we left
after four years I owed the bank five hundred
and all I had was three old mules, a pony,
and not one cow. I did have family though,
six boys and these two girls. Now this boy here,
he's going on twelve. Three years ago we left
our place in Oklahoma. Young as he was
I used to put him out behind a mule.
These girls plowed too. I start them young. We work
together. Out in the field my shadow amounts
to a whole lot. You ask them if it don't.
The girls when they come in at noon would grab
their hoes and tend the flower garden. Shore,
my girls did that when they were resting up
from busting out a field. We moved from there
to Wagoner County and took our debts along.
The bank was real obliging, turned me loose
but held me tight. The Wagoner bank took over.
We made a crop but lightning killed two mules
one night and then a cyclone hit through there.
It scared my horse so bad he run into
a tree and broke his neck. That left one mule.
I went to buying scrub stock then for ten
and fifteen dollars. I'd got down to where
my credit wasn't any good because
all my security was gone. About
that time the plow-up come. I told the man
the truth. Generally I raised forty
acres of cotton, sometimes fifty, had
the cotton hands in family for the work
and growing all the living that we had
to have. They caught the feller told the truth
and cut his acres down. I landed with

sixteen instead of forty. When they done that
the older children said, "No use for us
to stay on here. We'll have to hunt a job."
Two of them left. We never heard from them.
That fall we druv the truck to Texas, caught
the cotton picking, made expenses, come
back home no better off. So I put in
for one of them new farm security loans.
We had a bunch of chickens, milk cows and hogs
but we was short on feed. That winter was
real cold. Three hundred of my chickens starved.
You could go out and see them dropping dead.
We lost one mule, one cow, just on starvation.
You know, to a farmer that don't look good.
We got our government loan but not in time.
If I had got that loan to have bought feed
the first of January I could have put
them chickens to producing and went on.
So I says, "Well, now, this is our last crop.
I'll never see another thing of mine
die of starvation, not if I starve to death."
I made my crop, sold out – don't owe no banks –
paid up the government loan, and still had left
a dollar or two. We took a notion then
to leave, one morning loaded up some stuff,
eight head of us – six chaps and two grown folks –
into a roadster, Model A. We'd heard
that Gilbert, Arizona, was the place
where cotton really grew and you could make
good money in the fields, so we took off
down Sixty-six, through Amarillo, Texas,
and was it cold! December was the month.
We got to Gilbert but it wasn't like
they said. We lived in tents, right on the ground.

Them small-poxers, scabby as goats, would come
out in the field and pick. This girl caught it.
Her head was a solid scab. Here comes this school
feller. "She's got to be in school. You see
she's there tomorrow or it's jail for you."
We used to keep them out once in a while
to pick and help get up the grocery bill.
Here comes the health department bringing her back.
"Why did you send that girl to school? Don't you
know smallpox when you see it?" I told him why
I sent her. "Now the school is quarantined,
and this camp too. Nobody better leave."
They kept us quarantined for three whole weeks.
We couldn't even pick. They had to feed us.
When we got loose we went to Avondale
to pick. A barracks made of tin all full
of holes, that was our home, eight people in
one room. Early one morning my wife waked up.
She saw the next room through a great big hole.
A woman there was busy picking lice
off of her children. We got out and come
to California, to the government camp
at Calpat in the Imperial Valley. We
had showers. Things was all kept clean. We stayed
till that camp moved and then we moved with it.
We worked a while in peas best way we could.
Fifteen hundred people just in one field.
They wanted to pick peas so bad they'd fight
over a row. A hamper was the most
I ever picked. No one could live on that.
We went to Beaumont for the cherries. Then
we went up north to Thornton, worked in hay
a little, apricots in San Jose,
and back again to Thornton for tomatoes.

The Filipinos and Japanese
got all the good tomatoes which I guess
they knew how better than the average.
Visalia was the next place. There we chopped
cotton a while and then we tried Calpat
once more. I made hampers. When work give out
we went on back to Thornton. Here a while,
then some place else. We just keep moving on.
You reckon there's a home for us somewhere?
Somebody must could use a family.


ALTOGETHER SINGING

Dream of people altogether singing
each singing his way to self
to realms on realms within
all singing their way on out of self
singing through to unity
kindling into flame of common purpose from the
        altogether singing

such singing once I heard
where black children sang the chants of work in slavery
of hope for life at last and justice beyond the spaded
        unmarked grave
the platform dignitaries
of master race stooping for the occasion
were suddenly shamed and shaken
by these fierce and singing children
chanting out their stormy hunger
for freeborn rights
still wickedly denied

39   *Whose America?*

again once
in packed and stifling union hall
where miners gathered and their womenfolk
I heard such singing
while outside in the listening street
men stood uneasy and shivering beneath their heavy
     uniforms
more firmly gripped their guns
though unarmed were the singers
save for the weapon of song

and once again
where followers of the ripening crops
along that hot relentless valley hemmed by cool mirage
     of high Sierras
square danced with riotous feet
outstamping fiddlesqueak and banjo's tinny jingle
there came a quiet
and from the quiet
burst altogether singing
yearning back to lands whence these were driven
the known and homely acres
then lusting forward to the richness of unending rows
     and vines and groves
the treasure tended only
but some day to be taken and be rightly used
the prophecy sang forth

# II
## *1940*

# IN EGYPT LAND

# IN EGYPT LAND

## I

It was Alabama, 1932
but the spring came
same as it always had.
A man just couldn't help believing
this would be a good year for him
when he saw redbud and dogwood everywhere in bloom
and the peachtree blossoming
all by itself
up against the gray boards of the cabin.
A man had to believe
so Cliff James hitched up his pair of old mules
and went out and plowed up the old land
the other man's land but he plowed it
and when it was plowed it looked new again
the cotton and corn stalks turned under
the red clay shining with wet
under the sun.

Years ago
he thought he bought this land
borrowed the money to pay for it
from the furnish merchant in Notasulga
big white man named Mr Parker
but betwixt the interest and the bad times coming
Mr Parker had got the land back
and nigh on to $500 more owing to him
for interest seed fertilize and rations
with a mortgage on all the stock-
the two cows and their calves
the heifer and the pair of old mules-

Mr Parker could come drive them off the place any day
if he took a notion
and the law would back him.

Mighty few sharecroppers
black folks or white
ever got themselves stock like Cliff had
they didn't have any cows
they plowed with the landlord's mule and tools
they didn't have a thing.
Took a heap of doing without
to get your own stock and your own tools
but he'd done it
and still that hadn't made him satisfied.
The land he plowed
he wanted to be his.
Now all come of wanting his own land
he was back to where he started.
Any day
Mr Parker could run him off
drive away the mules the cows the heifer and the calves
to sell in town
take the wagon the plow tools the store-bought furniture
      and the shotgun
on the debt.
No
that was one thing Mr Parker never would get a hold of
not that shotgun. . .

Remembering that night last year
remembering the meeting
in the church he and his neighbors always went to
deep in the woods

and when the folks weren't singing or praying or
     clapping and stomping
you could hear the branch splashing over rocks
right out behind.
That meeting night
the preacher prayed a prayer
for all the sharecroppers
white and black
asking the good Lord Jesus
to look down
and see how they were suffering.
"Five cent cotton Lord
and no way Lord for a man to come out.
Fifty cents a day Lord for working in the field
just four bits Lord for a good strong hand
from dawn to dark Lord from can till can't
ain't no way Lord a man can come out.
They's got to be a way Lord show us the way. . . "
And then they sang.
"Go Down Moses" was the song they sang
"Go down Moses, way down in Egypt land
Tell old Pharaoh to let my people go"
and when they had sung the song
the preacher got up and he said
"Brothers and sisters
we got with us tonight
a colored lady teaches school in Birmingham
going to tell us about the Union
what's got room for colored folks and white
what's got room for all the folks
that ain't got no land
that ain't got no stock
that ain't got no something to eat half the year
that ain't got no shoes

45   *In Egypt Land*

that raises all the cotton
but can't get none to wear
'cept old patchedy overhauls and floursack dresses.
Brothers and sisters
listen to this colored lady from Birmingham
who the Lord done sent I do believe
to show us the way. . . "

Then the colored lady from Birmingham
got up and she told them.
She told them how she was raised on a farm herself
a sharecrop farm near Demopolis
and walked six miles to a one-room school
and six miles back every day
till her people moved to Birmingham
where there was a high school for colored
and she went to it.
Then she worked in white folks' houses
and saved what she made
to go to college.
She went to Tuskegee
and when she finished
got a job teaching school in Birmingham
but  she never could forget
the people she was raised with
the sharecrop farmers
and how they had to live.
No
all the time she was teaching school
she thought about them
what could she do for them
and what could they do for themselves.
Then one day
somebody told her about the Union. . .

If everybody joined the Union she said
a good strong hand would get what he was worth
a dollar (Amen sister)
instead of fifty cents a day.
At settling time the cropper could take his cotton to
      the gin
and get his own fair half and the cotton seed
instead of the landlord hauling it off and cheating on
      the weight.
"All you made was four bales Jim" when it really was six
(Ain't it God's truth?)
and the Union would get everybody the right to have
      a garden spot
not just cotton crowded up to the house
and the Union would see the children got a schoolbus
like the white children rode in every day
and didn't have to walk twelve miles.
That was the thing
the children getting to school
(Amen)
the children learning something besides chop cotton
      and pick it
(Yes)
the children learning how to read and write
(Amen)
the children knowing how to figure
so the landlord wouldn't be the only one
could keep accounts
(Preach the Word sister).

Then the door banging open against the wall
and the Laws in their lace boots
the High Sheriff himself
with his deputies behind him.

47   *In Egypt Land*

Folks scrambling to get away
out the windows and door
and the Laws' fists going *clunk clunk clunk*
on all the men's and women's faces they could reach
and when everybody was out and running
the pistols going off behind them.
Next meeting night
the men that had them brought shotguns to church
and the High Sheriff got a charge of birdshot in his body
when Ralph Gray with just his single barrel
stopped a car full of Laws
on the road to the church
and shot it out with their 44's.
Ralph Gray died
but the people in the church
all got away alive.


## II


The crop was laid by.
From now till picking time
only the hot sun worked
ripening the bolls
and men rested after the plowing and plowing
women rested
little boys rested
and little girls rested
after the chopping and chopping with their hoes.
Now the cotton was big.
Now the cotton could take care of itself from the weeds
while the August sun worked
ripening the bolls.

Cliff James couldn't remember ever making a better crop
on that old red land
he'd seen so much of
wash down the gullies toward the Tallapoosa
since he'd first put a plow to it.
Never a better crop
but it had taken the fertilize
and it had taken work
fighting the weeds
fighting the weevils. . .
Ten bales it looked like it would make
ten good bales when it was picked
a thousand dollars worth of cotton once
enough to pay out on seed and fertilize and furnish
        for the season
and the interest and something down
on the land
new shoes for the family to go to church in
work shirts and overalls for the man and boys
a bolt of calico for the woman and girls
and a little cash money for Christmas.


Now though
ten bales of cotton
didn't bring what three used to.
Two hundred and fifty dollars was about what his share
        of this year's crop would bring
at five cents a pound
not even enough to pay out on seed and fertilize and
        furnish for the season
let alone the interest on the land Mr Parker was asking
        for
and $80 more on the back debt owing to him.

Mr Parker had cut his groceries off at the commissary
      last month
and there had been empty bellies in Cliff James' house
with just cornbread buttermilk and greens to eat.
If he killed a calf to feed his family
Mr Parker could send him to the chain-gang
for slaughtering mortgaged stock.

Come settling time this fall
Mr Parker was going to get every last thing
every dime of the cotton money
the corn
the mules
the cattle
and the law would back him.
Cliff James wondered
why had he plowed the land in the spring
why had he worked and worked his crop
his wife and children alongside him in the field
and now pretty soon
they would all be going out again
dragging their long sacks
bending double in the hot sun
picking Mr Parker's cotton for him.

Sitting on the stoop of his cabin
with his legs hanging over the rotten board edges
Cliff James looked across his fields of thick green cotton
to the woods beyond
and a thunderhead piled high in the south
piled soft and white like cotton on the stoop
like a big day's pick
waiting for the wagon
to come haul it to the gin.

On the other side of those woods
was John McMullen's place
and over yonder just east of the woods
Ned Cobb's and beyond the rise of ground
Milo Bentley lived that was the only new man
to move into the Reeltown section that season.
Milo just drifted in from Detroit
because his work gave out up there
and a man had to feed his family
so he came back to the farm
thinking things were like they used to be
but he was finding out different.
Yes
everybody was finding out different
Cliff and John and Ned and Milo and Judson Simpson
    across the creek
even white croppers like Mr Sam and his brother Mr Bill
they were finding out.
It wasn't many years ago Mr Sam's children
would chunk at Cliff James' children
on their way home from school
and split little Cliff's head open with a rock once
because his daddy was getting too uppity
buying himself a farm.
Last time they had a Union meeting though at Milo
    Bentley's place
who should show up but Mr Sam and Mr Bill
and asked was it only for colored
or could white folks join
because something just had to be done
about the way things were.
When Cliff told them
it was for all the poor farmers
that wanted to stick together

they paid their nickel to sign up
and their two cents each for first month's dues
and they said they would try to get
more white folks in
because white men and black
were getting beat with the same stick these days.


Things looked worse than they ever had in all his time
    of life
Cliff James thought
but they looked better too
they looked better than they ever had in all his time
    of life
when a sharecropper like Ralph Gray
not drunk but cold sober
would stand off the High Sheriff with birdshot
and get himself plugged with 44's
just so the others at the meeting could get away
and after that the mob hunting for who started the Union
beating men and women up with pistol butts and bull
    whips
throwing them in jail and beating them up more
but still not stopping it
the Union going on
more people signing up
more and more every week
meeting in houses on the quiet
nobody giving it away
and now white folks coming in too.


Cliff James looked over his ripening cotton to the woods
and above the trees the thunderhead piled still higher
    in the south

white like a pile of cotton on the stoop
piling up higher and higher
coming out of the south
bringing storm. . .

### III

"You"
Cliff James said
"nor the High Sheriff
nor all his deputies
is gonna git them mules."
The head deputy put the writ of attachment back in his
      inside pocket
then his hand went to the butt of his pistol
but he didn't pull it.
"I'm going to get the High Sheriff and help"
he said
"and come back and kill you all in a pile."

Cliff James and Ned Cobb watched the deputy whirl
      the car around
and speed down the rough mud road.
He took the turn skidding
and was gone.
"He'll be back in a hour" Cliff James said
"if'n he don't wreck hisseff."
"Where you fixin' to go?" Ned Cobb asked him.
"I's fixin' to stay right where I is."
"I'll go git the others then."
"No need of eve'ybody gittin' kilt" Cliff James said.
"Better gittin' kilt quick
than perishin' slow like we been a'doin'" and Ned Cobb
      was gone

cutting across the wet red field full of dead cotton
    plants
and then he was in the woods
bare now except for the few green pines
and though Cliff couldn't see him
he could see him in his mind
calling out John McMullen and telling him about it
then cutting off east to Milo Bentley's
crossing the creek on the foot-log to Judson Simpson's. . .
Cliff couldn't see him
going to Mr Sam or Mr Bill about it
no
this was something you couldn't expect white folks to
    get in on
even white folks in your Union.


There came John McMullen out of the woods
toting that old musket of his.
He said it went back to Civil War days
and it looked it
but John could really knock a squirrel off a limb
or get a running rabbit with it.
"Here I is," John said
and "What you doin' 'bout you folks?"
"What folks?"
"The ones belongin' to you.
You chilrens and you wife,"
"I disremembered 'em," Cliff James said.
"I done clean disremembered all about my chilrens and
    my wife."
"They can stay with mine," John said.
"We ain't gonna want no womenfolks nor chilrens
not here we ain't."

Cliff James watched his family going across the field
the five backs going away from him
in the wet red clay among the dead cotton plants
and soon they would be in the woods
his wife
young Cliff
the two girls
and the small boy. . .
They would just have to get along
best way they could
because a man had to do
what he had to do
and if he kept thinking about the folks belonging to him
he couldn't do it
and then he wouldn't be any good to them
or himself either.
There they went into the woods
the folks belonging to him gone
gone for good
and they not knowing it
but he knowing it
yes God
he knowing it well.

When the head deputy got back
with three more deputies for help
but not the High Sheriff
there were forty men in Cliff James' cabin
all armed.
The head deputy and the others got out of the car
and started up the slope toward the cabin.
Behind the dark windows
the men they didn't know were there
sighted their guns.

55   *In Egypt Land*

Then the deputies stopped.
"You Cliff James!" the head deputy shouted
"come on out
we want to talk with you."
No answer from inside.
"Come on out Cliff
we got something we want to talk over."
Maybe they really did have something to talk over
Cliff James thought
maybe all those men inside
wouldn't have to die for him or he for them. . .
"I's goin' out," he said.
"No you ain't," Ned Cobb said.
"Yes I is," Cliff James said
and leaning his shotgun against the wall
he opened the door just a wide enough crack
for himself to get through
but Ned Cobb crowded in behind him
and came out too
without his gun
and shut the door.
Together they walked toward the Laws.
When they were halfway Cliff James stopped
and Ned stopped with him
and Cliff called out to the Laws
"I's ready to listen white folks".


"This is what we got to say nigger!"
and the head deputy whipped out his pistol.
The first shot got Ned
and the next two got Cliff in the back
as he was dragging Ned to the cabin.
When they were in the shooting started from inside

everybody crowding up to the windows
with their old shotguns and muskets
not minding the pistol bullets from the Laws.
Of a sudden John McMullen
broke out of the door
meaning to make a run for his house
and tell his and Cliff James' folks
to get a long way away
but a bullet got him in the head
and he fell on his face
among the dead cotton plants
and his life's blood soaked into the old red land.

The room was full of powder smoke and men groaning
that had caught pistol bullets
but not Cliff James.
He lay in the corner quiet
feeling the blood run down his back and legs
but when somebody shouted
"The Laws is runnin' away!"
he got to his feet and went to the door and opened it.
Sure enough three of the Laws
were helping the fourth one into the car
but it wasn't the head deputy.
There by the door-post was John McMullen's old musket
where he'd left it when he ran out and got killed.
Cliff picked it up and saw it was still loaded.
He raised it and steadied it against the door-post
aiming it at where the head deputy would be sitting
to drive the car.
Cliff only wished
he could shoot that thing like John McMullen. . .

He didn't know there was such a place in all Alabama
just for colored.
They put him in a room to himself
with a white bed and white sheets
and the black nurse put a white gown on his black body
after she washed off the dried black blood.
Then the black doctor came
and looked at the pistol bullet holes in his back
and put white bandages on
and stuck a long needle in his arm
and went away.

How long ago was it
he stayed and shot it out with the Laws?
Seemed like a long time
but come to think of it
he hid out in Mr Sam's corn crib
till the sun went down that evening
then walked and walked all the night-time
and when it started to get light he saw a cabin
with smoke coming out the chimney
but the woman wouldn't let him in to get warm
so he went on in the woods and lay down
under an old gum tree and covered himself with leaves
and when he woke up it was nearly night-time again
and there were six buzzards perched in the old gum tree
watching him. . .
Then he got up and shooed the buzzards away
and walked all the second night-time
and just as it was getting light
he was here

and this was Tuskegee
where the Laws couldn't find him
but John McMullen was dead in the cotton field
and the buzzards would be at him by now
if nobody hadn't buried him
and who would there be to bury him
with everybody shot or run away or hiding?


In a couple of days it was going to be Christmas
yes Christmas
and nobody belonging to Cliff James
was going to get a thing
not so much as an orange or a candy stick
for the littlest boy.
What kind of a Christmas was that
when a man didn't even have a few nickels
to get his children some oranges and candy sticks
what kind of a Christmas and what kind of a country
     anyway
when you made ten bales of cotton
five thousand pounds of cotton
with your own hands
and your wife's hands
and all your children's hands
and then the Laws came to take your mules away
and drive your cows to sell in town
and your calves
and your heifer
and you couldn't even get commissary credit
for coffee molasses and sow-belly
and nobody in your house had shoes to wear
or any kind of fitting Sunday clothes
and no Christmas for nobody. . .

"Go Down Moses" was the song they sang
and when they had finished singing
it was so quiet in the church
you could hear the branch splashing over rocks
right out behind.
Then the preacher got up and he preached. . .


"And there was a man what fought to save us all
he wropped an old quilt around him
because it was wintertime and he had two pistol bullets
     in his back
and he went out of his house
and he started walking across the country to Tuskegee.
He got mighty cold
and his bare feet pained him
and his back like to killed him
and he thought
here is a cabin with smoke coming out the chimley
and they will let me in to the fire
because they are just poor folks like me
and when I have got warm
I will be on my way to Tuskegee
but the woman was afeared
and barred the door again him
and he went and piled leaves over him in the woods
waiting for the night-time
and six buzzards settled in an old gum tree
watching did he still breathe. . . "


*The Sheriff removed Cliff James from the hospital to the county jail on December 22. A mob gathered to lynch the prisoner on Christmas day. For protection he was taken to jail in Montgomery. Here Cliff James died on the stone floor of his cell, December 27, 1932.*

# III

## *1941-1944*

## THEIR BLOOD
## CRIES OUT

# HERE I STAND

## I.

Starting from Alabama
on September 8, 1941
I came North
to find out what was going on
what people were thinking feeling getting ready to do or
        already doing
what I could do
more than I was already doing
which was not enough
not nearly enough.

The sun went down on Georgia
behind the silver speeding train.
The red eroded land
went black.
Only the black pines
and the gleam of kerosene in cabin windows
went by.

All through the night waking up
and the same South still
the black and jagged land
plow-wrecked, cashcrop-gutted, rained down to the sea
and the pines
like what's left of an army
straggling home from defeat.

This America
this part of America
this much of America

and what have we done with it?
what are we doing with it?
so the doing is bigger than the talk about doing?
this American South?

Here the last eight years of my life
have gone
working with people in lost unthought-of places
and what to show?
Eight years given up
the years that count
that fix the lines of a man
beyond any future unshaping
except he be hammered to pieces.

Aimed years these were
not years at random
sniffing tonguing this and that
but years like great shells hurled at their objective
or bombs dropped after sighting
years of my full strength
being fully used
and my strength grew the more it was called on.

I learned
that strength is a matter of the made-up mind
the knowing what is to be done
clenched with the will to do it
and the way then comes of itself
obstacles explode into rubble
enemies fall back.

This knowledge then to show
for eight years of going up against

what must be gone against everywhere
if we mean the words we are saying
and no armistice anywhere
least of all in Wilmington, Birmingham, Natchez and Belle
    Glade
places I know.

How shake off the sense of all this land?
not the South only
but all of it
from cut-over Maine and the fishermen
cursed by the sea's too great bounty
to fat Wisconsin sicklied over with debt
the Dakotas Oklahoma and Texas
where the dark winds blew people off along with the topsoil
and the tractors every year advance
pitiless as tanks
driving more people before them
out to Arizona and California
and the human tides flowing along the valleys
from Agua Fria Yuma Calipatria and Indio
following the cotton the lettuce and the peas
on up the San Joaquin to the Sacramento
and doubling back
all places I have been
things and people I have seen
how shake off the thought of them
or of hideous Baltimore and Philadelphia
street after hideous street
Youngstown Ohio where the mill smoke dirties the snow
    before it even hits the ground
bleak Butte Montana on its nude and tawny hills
poisoned with copper
or Paterson New Jersey?

Silken things shimmer behind Fifth Avenue's acres of plate
    glass a few miles away
but there is no shimmer to Paterson
the silk mills boarded up
the empty streets
the corner loafers
the ugly words chalked on the vacant walls
the smell of stale sweat
(it will not out)
and the grimy quiet.

Aware of this in blood and bone
going to sleep with it
waking up with it
how change
how shake off the sense
of what there is to do
in the here
in the now?
not in any tomorrow
not across distant seas
so easy to promise
mongering words
but mark you
the stink of the lie sticks to the unfelt word
the slick restatement of what proved itself empty
once
and will again.

This is the ax
at the root of faith
this the sharp edge of disbelief.

II.

Pulling out of Alexandria
and the drunk in the washroom
lurching and weaving between the shiny bowls
trying to get something off his mind.
He bossed 150 men on a defense job
powder plant arsenal or dam
he didn't make it clear
but what he didn't like
he was sure of.

The blueprints
they made it go round and round
when it ought to go straight
the thing was to get this thing built
not some guy show how smart he was
and the government ought to know about this
no sense to it
no sense at all in going all around a thing
instead of straight through
and he was going to tell the government about it.

"Kill 'em
just kill about twelve of them Germans
the right twelve
and it'd be all over.
You oughtn't to go against
the working sort of people
no time
nowhere."

The silver train on the Potomac bridge
and the city ahead

the dome the shaft the shining sunlit blocks
and the drunk straddled at the window
"Washntn" he reverently says
"Thass my town
Washntn D. C."

III.

Along the stately tedious corridors
in anterooms to air-conditioned offices
        (the administrator will see you in a few minutes)
the rugs so soft after sidewalk and tile
sinking down upon soothing and pliable leather
creamy the walls with a slum scene in pastel
and a leader's picture
inscribed
there the obsession returns
the strength-killing word
DECEMBER
over and over again going round
like a victrola record caught in one groove
DECEMBER DECEMBER DECEMBER
what day is today?
a day in December
and tomorrow?
another day in December.
(But it's really September
October comes next and then all of November.)
But that was August, August last year
and coming back to my hotel from being out with people
he stepped from the shadows and touched my arm.
"You remember me?"
Small, stooping, Jewish,
thick glasses making his big eyes bigger

red hair like the outside sign of a deep inward smolder.
Ten years it had been
he then a student in college
I an instructor
and here he was
appearing out of the sultry night of a Washington August
the man with a month for a name
the month when the last leaves fall
in the sleety wind
and the limbs branch black
against the gray sky.
We sat on a bench in the little square facing my hotel
        and he said
"You have influence
you know people
maybe you can help me."
"I hope so" I told him calling him by the month which was
also his name.
"I've written a book" he said "the only book that's been
written on the topic" and he told me about it.
"We need a book on that" I said. "There hasn't been a book
on it and there ought to be."
"But I can't get it published" he said. "They tell me it
wouldn't make money. If I can get $500 from some foundation
they'll publish it. I thought maybe you could help me. You
know so many people."
"Yes" I said "I know a great many people. But I have a book
too which I can't get anybody to publish because they think
it wouldn't sell. Not now. Not while everybody is interest-
ed in something else and wanting to forget about our prob-
lems here at home. I can't help myself, so I don't see how
there's much chance of my helping you."
"But I put so much into it" he said.
"And so did I into mine" I said.

"I have a little job here and my wife has" he said "relief jobs
and all the time off the job I put on my book
nights and Saturday afternoons and Sundays
two years steady
and now I can't get it published because it wouldn't make
money." "Yes" I said "that's the way it seems to be."

IV.

My friend's voice was warm over the telephone
full of friendship
not to be doubted
"John" he said
"of course we can use you and we will use you if you say so."
"I am saying so" I said "I want to be used
I need to be used
please use me where I can be used."
"John" he said "we can only use 60 per cent of you in the
      government
and you want to give 120
you always have given us that
suppose we put you to work
in five or six months you won't be satisfied
you won't be able to stand the limitations
what you need is a really big job
nothing less will hold you."
"Stop buttering me up" I said.
"I mean it" he said. "You're too creative for the govern-
      ment."

And so, after ten days of going from office to office
I get the truth.
Not wanted.
Oh, in a last extremity, my money all gone, needing to

eat, yes,
but my need
not theirs
not my country's.

It is something to get this stated
something to get it in words
worth all the days
of not coming to grips
of sensing the friendship
but sensing also something else
(go somewhere else with your gab and your loitering
Mr. Whitman
and your great concerns
for you make us uncomfortable
and we must get on with our small ones.)

Oh, admitting the importance of detail
and nobody ever paid more attention to detail than I
still there must be something else
and to think that at this time of times
that something else is feared
(the administrator will see you in a few minutes.)

Who I am
is neither here nor there
but that the words could be said. . .
"too creative"
meaning
too full of the seed from which new things grow.

Seed.
The new thing springing.
Though young

I have four children
and I was not uninstructed.
That was all part of it
and I couldn't be careful
or if careful beforehand
the rage of the blood
the unstoppable thing
burst through the dam
in spring flood.

The earth
the wonderful womanly earth
and how can the rain withhold itself
or the seed not plunge
deep into sheath?

I was not prudent.
Prudent in nothing
and when the bridge was before me
the stanchions rising into fog
I took it
across the far below water.

Unthinkable, what we were about to do
but I did not think
(for how can the rain withhold itself
or the seed not plunge?)
and we came to the very ends of the earth
the uttermost point
where the sea beat under
and stairs went down from the lonely beacon
(Drake touched here in the long ago
and we, it seemed, were the next.)
All night around the cabin

the vast Pacific pines dripped on the earth.

May it was
May the next
and the kissed earth quivered
blood beading the white
(who could understand
so right and so wrong?)

White of blossoms of marble and of linen waiting
the dark and pillowed hair
the furious compact
sealed in blood.

(Would that the prow of the Argonauts
had never passed between the dark and moving-together
　　rocks
toward the land of the golden fleece
nor in the forests of Pelion had ever the pines been felled
to make the oars)

V.

Three minutes to catch the five o'clock for New York
and there at the ticket window
he stands in line before me
the man with a month for a name
and somehow I am not surprised
nor am I surprised that we are going the same way by the
　　same train.

When we are seated and the dome the shaft the shining
　　sunlit blocks fly backwards
so soft the power in the stored wires

the streets yards roundhouses Maryland hills and fields
    do the moving
while the train is cradled still.

"Has your book been published?" I ask him.
"No. Has yours?"
"No."

He has lost his job in Washington, a relief job that played
    out and though hundreds are being hired every day
    he somehow cannot be used any more
and his wife has lost her job also for belonging to some-
    thing she had a right to belong to according to the
    precious charter of American liberties but in order
    to defend these the better the authorities are finding
    it expedient to abridge them in certain instances.

Nevertheless in every instance life must go on.
Skating rinks, these days, by contrast to treatises on
    domestic social questions, make money, despite the
    preoccupation of the populace with foreign affairs.
The possibilities of establishing a new skating rink in
    Baltimore, he has been told, are good
and he is on his way there to investigate them unless,
    perchance, I can suggest a better idea
which I at the moment
cannot.

Baltimore flies backward
the red identical rows of houses with white identical steps
    to the sidewalk
the aircraft plant raw and stupendous
with 150 bombers for lack of propellers
ranged helpless on the field

(give pots and pans for propellers)
and no skating rink in evidence.

Next stop
30th Street
(the 30th day)
Philadelphia
(of December)
december december december december
the dark land flying backwards
then lit streets flicking
great shipyard cranes rising into darkness
glimpse of plastic firehearted metal under enormous
    forging hammer
furnace pallor neon sheen and the rails speeding backward
    alongside and silver
the trucks on the joints insisting december december. . .

VI.

The black girl on the bare wall
looks down
a trophy she and a talisman
sole spoils from a lost battle
lips nose thick and the kinky hair braided
but from behind this adventitious mask
all women look out
and you who saw behind the mask and drew the essence
drawing yourself in doing so
and all dear women
the love
the woman being loved and loving
each time and each one always the first one and the first
    time

(ever virgin)

outside my ninth floor cell
the lights climb up and up
the el streaks like a strict and luminous ruler athwart
the monstrous highpiled blocks

next morning Sunday
and the free air moves in the uninfested glittering un-
        believable avenue
on into the park
where side by side
hyena and puma are caged
the loping cringe of the one incessant and stricken
somewhere a lion roars and terror shakes the carrion beast
the downslanted hindquarters cower lower
the black and scalded privates quivering contract
then having dunged
the thing resumes his lope
but the puma
unshakably seated
the head high the furred neck and shoulders superb
the marvelous muscles in repose
the eyes green-gray and straight to the front
looking through cages through people through monstrous
        high-piled blocks
and from time to time
the lifted lips
the white-fanged hiss
bespeaking the will never to feed
upon the lion's leavings
nor to pick the bones of the carcass
left behind by the sated wolf.

# VII.

"They've turned art into a whorehouse" he said
"not a real whorehouse but a pseudo whorehouse
if it were a real one that would be different
that would be all right.
But here in America
they buy and sell the artist
and then don't use him."

The old man on the couch was speaking
speaking not exactly to me but through me
the furious and undaunted eyes like the eyes of the puma
though dark and plumbless.
"Your friend who drew the head of this black girl
is an artist
you say she works at her art and will not give up
(she will be successful)
but when success comes
do you think she can stand it?
I have seen so many young people
with the gift of seeing and the fidelity to put down what
        they saw just as they saw it
and then they succeed
and that is the end of them."

"I think she will be able to stand it" I said.

"You never know" he said. "The pressure is terrible.
        America corrupts her best and puts them to no use. A
        few stand out against it. Only a few."

The puma does not range his cage but sits
and in his sitting is more life compact

77   *Their Blood Cries Out*

than in the hyena's ceaseless circling.
The puma sits not having space to spring.


Hair sprouts from the old man's ears like tasseled corn in
    sunlight
but in the newspaper office
(tall temple of liberty, multistoried fane)
December closes back
with the close-lipped man
moulder of popular opinion
who reads the letter presenting me
and then says
"I can think of nothing."
But I am thinking of something
I am thinking how this close-lipped man
having as much as any other perhaps
created a certain climate of opinion
a certain popular skepticism about slogans and crusades
has now reversed himself and must likewise reverse the
    public mind.
He does not seem to me a happy man
or a man conscious of any presence but his own, and
    that unwelcome.
Was I wrong then, he must be thinking,
(through my fault through my fault through my most
    grievous fault) and am I right now?
Or am I wrong now (the pressure is terrible) though right
    then and what will be the judgment upon me?
Or right both then and now? (The circumstances are
    entirely different.)
Or both times wrong? (Things are always mixed. Every
    slogan is partly true and partly false. Every crusade is
    partly a high emprise and partly a piratical
    expedition.)

Why do I feel compassion for this successful man
who quite obviously feels none for me
though my formed and confident powers should rot in
    disuse?
Go away please and leave me alone with my two selves
he would be thinking if his thinking were entirely honest
or with my one half-self whichever it is
for the two must be made one
or the half whole
and there is no time to be lost

circling his cage

### VIII.

You could join the Canadian army
I say to myself
and while the ravens provide for your wife and children
shoot craps on a blanket for ha'pennies

### IX.

We dance upon the striped hide of a zebra
while the phonograph plays "Tuxedo Junction"
and I tell her about how I was shot at in Tuxedo
    Junction at twelve years of age
the other boy not liking the looks of me and coveting my
    new bicycle.
Twice his 22 cracked but both times he missed me.
Again once while still a boy I was the object of target
    practice through being mistaken for a Negro in the
    dark.
Four times the man shot and four times the heavy caliber
    slugs

79   *Their Blood Cries Out*

spat in the grass of the terrace I scrouged up to.

Time moves on to Mozart and we sit
while in the next room the voice of the man who was born
 to be a bishop
excathedrates with a corpulent catch at the close of each
 breath.
He categorically hopes (if that be possible) the lousy
 Russians and Germans kill one another off
tens of millions of lives being but a just price to pay
for submitting to bad leadership.
(For lo I have lifted my hand against the working sort of
 people.)
The plainclothes bishop taking himself canonically off to bed
 upon the stroke of twelve
for he must prepare copy betimes in the morning
having a deadline to meet
and millions wait upon his words
indeed a whole hemisphere
for thousands at his bidding speed
and post o'er land and ocean
waiting diesels throb and the vast motors of planes warm
 for the spuming take-off from blue Biscayne
and so he and his Jehovah to bed
but I linger
for she I sense
has something to say to me.

"I am a happy person
and I have been happy ever since one time in Shanghai
God spoke to me
God really did
and He told me everything was going to be all right

that in fact it was always all right
and He would never leave my side.

"In thirteen months
in a year from October
I shall go back to South Africa
if Hitler is not there before me
and I don't think he will be
do you?"

"No."

"I don't know why I should want to get away from New
     York
I make more money than I know what to do with
I have this lovely apartment
friends
everything I used to believe I wanted
but I keep thinking about South Africa."

"But why South Africa?"

"It's so free" this woman from Kansas tells me. "It's the freest
     place in the world."

                    X.

Across the screen the stiff and puppet people go
Sovkino's heroic proletarian as like to life as Hercules to me.
"Vodka vodka I must have vodka"
shouts the stagy bearded father
and breaks a strike to get it
while the fiendish bossmen gloat in their mustachios
to see the workers' blood

*81    Their Blood Cries Out*

a short follows
exhibiting the earthly relics and mementos of one P.
    Chaikovsky
"the ingenious P. Chaikovsky"
a composer of pre-revolutionary times but still a Russian.
We see the P. Chaikovsky museum
his wooden villa mid-Muscovite-Victorian
within doors the bust of P. Chaikovsky
(one almost smells the bayrum on the lifelike whiskers)
the creaking superfluous furniture
the crinkled, yellowed scores on the piano
and capping all
the silk hat with elegant gloves of P. Chaikovsky

and is that all that stays?

suddenly through the door they come
a troop of people
no proletarian heroes these nor vodka-shouters
but real
their imperfections writ large upon them
their yearnings also —
the heavy peasant forehead and the lips agape
(here dwelt the ingenious P. Chaikovsky, sainted man of
    music)
struggling to absorb the mystic influence from the holy
    ikons
silk hat with elegant gloves crinkled yellowed scores and
    bust
wanting the thing that is not here

the others
a boy in gunboat shoes scuffling and abashed
(like my boy David)

a clodlike girl with litten eyes
two shavenheaded men in Red Army blouses and starred
    caps in knotted hands
then all at once the music of the Pathetique
the ageless pain
bursting from the sound-track
existing from and by itself
shoulderblades crawl and needles penetrate the spine
the woe
ye who are about to die
or live far worse than dying
peasant forehead with your lips agape
scuffling boy like my boy David
girl with litten eyes
Red Army men
I salute you
wild with all regret the music and within me
I salute you
race humaine

## XI.

ever virgin
she is coming toward me
across vast breadth of earth
night of stars above and stars under
stars unmoving and changeless above
stars under single or clustered or nebulae
hued cuprous bloodred whiteblue of ladled steel green like
    first shoots pricking erect from the soil in spring
a whole arc of the world swinging under
tiny winking star by itself where the farmer rouses him-
    self and lighting his smoky lamp commences his

long day
cuprous sun where the jook-joint stays open all night
the soldier and the coal-heaver start for each other with
    beer bottles
the bouncer goes to work with his blackjack
and the unmilked slut pukes all over the table

twin beams on the highway delicate gemini
cross-country truck thunderous and huge
at the wheel the man awake aware
muscled controlled master of tons powered with wheels
or backseat lovers returning
all glandular tension relieved
the commemorative handkerchief dropped by the roadside
and the consummation by finger

constellation of a town
blue-windowed mill where spindles twirl
and weary women watch
pushing back their raveling hair from hungry hatchet faces
gas-stations lunch-wagons and the vacant main street beaded
the felt legion of the tired sleeping
the dome the shaft the shrouded unlit blocks
tilted up to window and circling slow and nearer
sad Lincoln watching and the pool reflecting

the hushed remote descent and muffled stop

(she does not live here. . . caged in this below. . .
    where minutes tick)

roaring it eats the field
earthfast planes hangars trees go storming by
now tail up and triumphantly thundering

until soft upon air it rests
and freely mounts
the earth swinging easily under

over white waves and rolling breakers of fog
the sun gleaming on them
and on wings of riveted silver
quivering in the rush of unseen air
she is coming toward me
ever virgin

the city is washed in fog
great buildings push up
tops lost in the moist
the morning Sunday-still
still almost as woods as vast Pacific pines
dripping on the earth

(and how can the rain withhold itself
or the seed not plunge?)

it is sixteen years since the whippoorwill sang in the pines
"Moonwinx" the place is called now with cabins and beer
        and a nickelodeon outblaring the whippoorwill
but one must never return to a once hallowed ground
never go back to recapture
going onward always

ever virgin
ever new
birth-pangs you have known four times through me
and yet
the wonder
insatiable the need

85   *Their Blood Cries Out*

for sixteen years I have explored this precious land
its lovely hills and valleys
gentle moulded vistas
dark woods and streams
and still when I debark upon its shore
coming home from Colchis
as fresh it is as sweet as fragrant with all right smells of earth
as sixteen years ago when first I planted standard here

ever virgin

you wept
when the milk would not come the last time
and your tears were hot as nitric acid
spilled over me once and my shoes shrivelled my socks
    plucked off in flakes
and on my eaten flesh the bare and branching veins were
    plain as winter trees against the sky.
Those scars I carry yet but the acid of your tears burnt deeper

through my most grievous fault

            but, by all above,
these blenches gave my heart another youth

home
the always unknown place
that must be known in whole and part
so known that no small bit escapes or ever shall
known to thinking seeing touching hearing smelling tasting
    brain
through eyes lips tongue teeth nose ears fingers toes and
    every end of nerve in skin that gladly would be flayed
to know the closer

## XII.

Coming four flights down from the borrowed room the
    fog has lifted
and the block lies quiet in the sunshine
next door there is a tree
imagine
a tree shadowing the pavement
and under it
as under his own vine and figtree
sits the owner of the property
FURNISHED ROOMS
and bright blue paint on doors on window frames
with view of tree

we advance and ask

"nah" he smirking says
"no room for you"
(for such as you implied)

"you aren't imagining things?" I question

"nah nah"

"then where can we find a room?"
(with blue on door and window frames implied and view of
    tree)

he didn't know he couldn't say in all New York
not there
most positively not
nah nah

and then the mirth of it
the wonderful and unintended compliment
comes home
and arms on curve of other's hip we go
laughing up the sunlit street
to think
that after sixteen years
fifteen in lawful wedlock
with christened children four
we can be taken for adulterers
so happy we so suspect to the public eye


XIII.


after the grim dark tunneling grind
at 125th the three get on
glowing from the sun
collars open armpits ringed with wet
two have poking sheaves of fishpoles
one a basket
the Irishman just right
poised on the perilous crest
(another drink would send him spiraling down)

the torpid subway car awakes
Irishman adjusts his poles with antic care
once, he says, he poked them in a fan
and hell to pay
with dust and stuff all over everybody

the gray-haired spinster next him at the window
turns a face no longer gray and pinched
but full of love, a lovely face, upon him
and down the aisle a little boy leans out to see and hear

unspoken the question of all the car
all the car wondering
what did you guys catch
out in the sun on the cool salt water
and heard old Triton blow his wreathed horn?

he of the basket senses the question
and with all simulated pomp
with mock and priestly ceremony
opens wide the lid of wicker
drawing forth a crab
a huge and well-clawed crab
and waves him in the aisle
but the poor dead crab
does not respond
the limp dead flippers dangle
and the claws hang listless down

this crab died that we might live
peace be unto his fierce and tameless soul
could a crab wish peace
but the sight of him there
the armored corpse
ivory mottling into red
sends salt and sunwashed air through all the car

XIV.

Pell-mell rushing down the steps
hold the door back and we are on
the subway starts the columns flicker past
and the smooth dark tunnel flows along

uptown though not down

89   *Their Blood Cries Out*

as we meant to go
so off at the next station up to the street across and down
    into the fetid glow
the wait long and (pardon me, madam, I wish to make a
    purchase) nothing to do but read the advertisements
then back to Grand Central

the sign not seen until doors closed behind us and the
    local resuming its grind
EXPRESS TRAINS NOT RUNNING
alone then under the tireless lights
except for the drunk asleep on the steps
(prickle at the base of the brain
are you a man?
now it will be seen)

Slowly the cast assembles
first a slender youth with curly hair
schooled to law and order he awakens the drunk on the
    steps
it is not permitted he softly warns
and the drunk erupts into noise
then lights a cigarette
which likewise is not permitted
but the slender youth with curly hair
edges discreetly away
two couples appear
making with us
three couples
all minding our own business

the drunk staggers to his feet

plan of campaign:

a right to the jaw
and left to the sodden belly
should he still show fight
160 pounds at him from ten paces
knee to the groin
then thumbs in the eyepits
hammering skull on concrete

his first quarry couple number one
he approaches them and they flush to the next bay
whereupon he deploys against couple number two
the male leads the retreat
looking unmanned
his female some paces behind
our turn now
and the drunk starts over
halfway I meet him
and he wavers to a stop

campaign plan or no
you can't hit such a thing

stiff-armed at the junction of neck and chin
with all power and no warning he topples backward
then quietly and without a word of remonstrance
goes away with recovered equilibrium
under the tireless lights the mute cast watches
until the appeaser
the slender youth with curly hair
takes charge
rushing to soothe the aggressor

soon querulous words are heard
"I wasn't doing a thing to him"

"He just came up and knocked the hell out of me"
"He wanted to kill me"
then the drunk to me
"You're tough, aren't you?"
"Where you're concerned" I say "yes I'm tough."
"When that subway train comes" he says from over his bay
    in the arms of the appeaser
"and we get on, I'm going to punch you right in the nose."
"Punch here, where the punching is good" I suggest and
    come over, sick at heart, but ready.
No answering move or word from his corner
I return to my wife and take from her
the papers I gave her to hold

again it begins
the wounded words
"I wasn't doing a thing to him"
and the appeaser comes over to us
"You better move on" he says
"he's drunk and you can't do anything with him
he'll heckle you as long as you stand here."

"Let him heckle" I say "but he'd better do his heckling
    from where he is."
"If I were you" the appeaser says "I'd move on."
"I'm not moving" I say.
The mute cast watches under the tireless lights
and the train coming we board it at the exact point where
    we've been waiting
except for the drunk
who gets on the car ahead

back in the room I wash and wash
the hand that touched him

## XV

Through the warm days
brightened by sun
and the warm nights
suffused by moon
insatiable love seeking solitude
companionship seeking crowds
and both were found in full measure

the lost
if lost
refound and more

he of the black palm
the once powerful
now all lips and lungs
roaring in bars
shhh from all sides shhh he hears
"I don't know whether you are brother and sister"
he said — "God love ye —
or husband and wife."

"We've been married a long time" we told him.

"Then get on the Third Avenue El" he told us.
"I can take you places they'd kill you for a nickel
this town is corrupt
but me I'm a human being
I like to see things growing
things pushing up
get on the Third Avenue El
and go out to the park
56 blocks of it

93   *Their Blood Cries Out*

look at the swans
and you'll get married all over again"

waving his huge and flabby arms
huge from digging anthracite in Shamokin Pennsylvania
flabby from lifting glasses in New York bars
("Ale" he said roaring "don't give me any of your beer")
he staggers across Fourteenth Street
stopping traffic with his black imperative palm

    so quickly they go
    the days and nights of warmth

    this thought is as a death, which cannot choose
    but weep to have that which it fears to lose

    and again alone

    MAN NOT WANTED

    men who can do what is wanted done
    in this town
    are a dime a dozen
    on a falling market
    sell yourself sell yourself sell yourself
    and be not used

    Here I stand
    John Beecher on the block
    sound of wind and limb and fully formed
    fit to bear the burden of my time
    until my spine cracks under the weight

    Do I hear any bids?

# JOSIAH TURNBULL TOOK NO PART IN POLITICS

Josiah Turnbull took no part in politics
toasting by the stove there
in his snug Philadelphia parlor
while the blizzard swirled
against the frosted panes
yes he congratulated himself
that he hadn't got mixed up
in anything political
but just attended to his own business

I wish I had lived in ancient Rome
in the days of the Gracchi
Josiah thought closing his Plutarch
ah with what dignity
the noble Romans went to their deaths
for their political beliefs
for liberty and justice
verily
Josiah thought knocking the ashes from his pipe
we have fallen upon evil days
and it behooves a man
to hold aloof
from the brawl in the marketplace
as I have done. . .

The door opened from the street
and a blast of cold
swept in from the hall
bending the lamp flames
Josiah could hear the redcoat Major
stamping the snow from his boots very carefully
before going upstairs to his room

the Major was always so correct
it was no hardship at all
to have him billeted there
and he paid for his lodging in gold

not like these Continentals
mechanics and country louts in stinking rags
with no gold or even silver to their names
but only paper
dirty worthless paper money
"not worth a Continental"
yes whatever the rights and wrongs of it might be
and there was much to be said on both sides
the British were the ones to do business with
and that very day
Josiah had made a most profitable bargain
with the British quartermaster
to deliver meat and grain for the garrison

there was the risk always
that the starving Continentals
encamped at the Valley Forge
might make a foray from their lair
and seize the farmers' wagons on the road
but it was Josiah's policy
to pay the farmers
only upon delivery of their produce in the city
so he did not stand to lose
whatever befell. . .

Josiah Turnbull stretched and yawned deeply
in his snug Philadelphia parlor
comfortably reflecting
that he took no part in politics

## AFTER EIGHTY YEARS

### I

Lincoln was pushed into it
they are still telling us
yes
after eighty years
they are still handing us that

I'd put it this way
Lincoln was just slow to catch on
slow to take hold
like many another man
trusting the experts but not himself fully
not really believing
in what he was fighting for
because he hadn't made his own mind up

Once Lincoln made his mind up
and wrote:
"thenceforward and forever free"
he started being the Lincoln we remember
and the war for Union
turned into a people's war
that could not be lost
Emancipation
kept England off the South's side
because the English working people
could not be made to fight for slavery

Emancipation
brought the Negroes in on the North's side
and turned the scale

Lincoln said so then
but after eighty years our school history books
still have nothing to say
about the 200,000 Negro soldiers and sailors
who lost a third of their number
fighting for their freedom and the Union
while the South warned
"none will be taken prisoners."
A Memphis slavedealer turned general
Nathan Bedford Forrest
captured Fort Pillow on the Mississippi
having ten men to the Union's one
and there under the white flags of surrender
bayoneted to death or buried alive
the Negro wounded
penned the Negro prisoners in wooden buildings
then burned them down
It was another story
at Port Hudson, Ship Island, Fort Wagner and
    Nashville
where Negroes fought on even terms
and it was a far different story
that day in 1865
when black cavalry rode into Richmond
at the head of Grant's army.
Behind these black fighters
were black workers for freedom
in hundreds of thousands
on the docks where munitions were unloaded
on Union fortifications from the Red River to the
    James and Potomac
builders teamsters cooks and nurses of the wounded
while by the hundreds of thousands
Negroes left their plows in the fields of slavery

seeking refuge in the camps of the blue armies
seeking work in freed fields
then having found it
they plowed to feed and clothe blue armies
while gray armies
went bare and hungry
After eighty years
we ought to know these things
better than we do

II

Eighty years
are a long while to be waiting
for somebody to finish
what Lincoln began.

Starting in 1863
Negro Americans with their own blood and toil
have bought and paid for freedom
full and unconditional
ten times over
and now in 1943
Negro Americans
in the army and the navy
by the hundreds of thousands
are fighting for the world's freedom
as well as their own. . .

In Lowndes County Alabama
Negroes are more than 85 per cent of all the people
but in all that county
not one Negro votes
not one Negro is called Mister by white people

and the few Negroes who own land
don't dare build themselves decent homes
for fear the white folks would resent it.
I saw a tumbledown tenant cabin in Lowndes
from which three dark boys had gone North
two of them are college deans now and the third
      a scientist

A few years back
the sharecroppers down in Lowndes tried to
      organize
because somebody from the outside
came in and told them
the President of the United States said they had a
      right to.
They counted the bodies they found afterward
the ones shot on dry land
and the ones that washed up bound hand and foot
on the Alabama River bank
but there were plenty still missing.
One planter told me
he'd been merciful himself
he just called a meeting of his croppers
in the church
and publicly whipped
the two or three that got mixed up in the union
that taught the rest of them a lesson
he told me

Between 1935 and 1940
400,000 farms were wiped off the southern map
400,000 families had to pull up stakes
more than 2,000,000 people cut adrift.
You've heard about the white farmers

from Oklahoma, Texas and Arkansas
and who went to California
and maybe you saw "The Grapes of Wrath"
but did you know
40,000 families were tractored out in Alabama
mostly Negroes
more people than lost out in Oklahoma?

No
we don't hear about them
nor about the 35,000 families in Georgia
who lost their chance to make a crop
they were mostly Negroes too

Where they all went
nobody exactly knows
some lived on where they were
in their little shacks and cabins
catching what wagehand work there was
sixty cents a day from can till can't
or picking cotton at 75c a hundred
some moved to town and went on relief
some hit the migrant trails
from Louisiana up through Arkansas and Kentucky
        on into Michigan
from Florida on up the coast to Lake Ontario and
        Maine

I got to know these people
down in Florida
and I would like to say something about them

They were living on the canal banks
in stinking quarters and barracks

sometimes thirteen people in a room
or in tarpaper huts and shelters in the weeds
and every morning before dawn came
they climbed on to trucks in the quarters
bound for the beanfields
where all day
everybody that could pick
down to the five and six year olds
picked
kneeling in the black Everglades muck.
It would be dark night again
when they got back to quarters
and all night long
the jook joints stayed open
so whiskey dice and women
could eat up the earnings of the day

That was the white growers' idea
of how to hold labor—
keep the Negroes broke
they said
and instead of a church or a school
a grower would build a jook joint
at the center of his quarters
to get back at night
what he paid out in the day

When the government came in
and started building a model camp for the Negroes
with screened shelters and shower baths
    and flush toilets
an infirmary a community center a school and
    playgrounds
laundry tubs and electric irons

the growers raised hell
what was the government's idea anyway
ruining the rental value of their canal bank
    quarters
and fixing to ruin their labor with a lot of useless
    luxury
besides the Negroes wouldn't use the camp
they liked to be dirty
they liked to be diseased
they liked to be vicious

When the growers saw
the government was going ahead anyway
they said
"You will have to hire a bunch of camp guards
white men
and have them patrol the camp
with clubs and pistols
or the Negroes
won't pay the rent
they will stop working entirely
and they will take the camp to pieces"

Let me tell you what happened
I know
because I was there
and I was in charge of the camp

When the day came to open
we just opened the gate
and let anybody in that wanted to come in
no hand-picking no references or anything like
    that
it was enough for us

that a family wanted to live there
and not on the canal bank

We didn't hire any white guards either
and nobody carried a club or a pistol
in all that camp that held a thousand people

We just got them altogether in the community
    center
and told them it was their camp
and they could make it a bad camp
or they could make it a good camp
that was up to them
and there wouldn't be any laws or ordinances
except the ones they made for themselves
through their elected council

Then for a week
they had a campaign in camp
with people running for office the first time in their
    lives
and after the campaign
people voted for the people they wanted to repre-
    sent them
for the first time in their lives
and after it was over
they celebrated with a big dance in the community
    center
and nobody got drunk and disorderly
and nobody cut anybody with a knife
and the only reason was
they had themselves a Council. . .
after that
the Council made the laws and ordinances

Council said
nobody's dog could run around loose
he had to be tied up
Council said
a man couldn't beat his wife up in camp
and when a man came in drunk one night and did
he was out of camp by morning
Council said
people had to pay their rent
because out of that rent money
came camp baseball equipment
and it kept up the nursery school
so when people wouldn't pay
Council put them out. . .
finally Council said
it's a long way to any store
we ought to have our own store
and that's how the co-op started
without a dollar in it
the people didn't put up. . .

Some of the men and women on that Council
couldn't so much as write their names
remember these were just country Negroes
off sharecrop farms in Georgia and Alabama
just common ordinary cottonpickers
the kind
Lowndes County planters say
would ruin the country
if they had the vote. . .

All I know is
my eyes have seen
democracy work

III

Freedom
is a whole lot more
than just not being owned by somebody.
Lincoln knew that.

Freedom starts with not being owned
but it also means
having a say in how you are governed
a home you can call yours
land if you're a farmer
that you can stay on year after year
hold it and improve it and get the benefit of it
either working for yourself alone
or a lot of farmers altogether working one big farm
for the good of all
and freedom means if you're a worker
the chance to learn the job of your choice
and the right to work at that job

Now
the United States government is putting up hun-
      dreds of millions of dollars
to teach new trades to citizens
both men and women
so they can build the planes the tanks the ships and
      guns
we must have to win
I was down in Georgia
looking over this government training program
and I saw fine new shops
full of the most uptodate machinery
millions of dollars worth

*106   HEAR THE WIND BLOW!*

and I saw where thousands of white people
men and women
were being taught at the expense of the government
how to weld ships and rivet airplanes and the rest
but I didn't see any Negroes in the shops
though Negroes are more than one out of every
        three
of Georgia's people
so I asked where were they. . .
this was kind of embarrassing to the authorities
they admitted they weren't training many
and said the reason was
the Negroes couldn't get jobs
even if they were trained
so there wasn't any use training them. . .

I had to go a long way in Georgia
to find any Negroes getting training
and when I found them
this is what I saw. . .
bare classrooms with benches and blackboards
not a lathe nor a drill press nor a welding machine
        in the place
men trying to learn through their eyes
what could only be learned through their hands

In all of Georgia
not one Negro woman
was getting even this kind of training
and when I asked why not
the authorities said to me surprised
"If Negro women could get war jobs
what would people do for cooks?"

Then there were the Negro carpenters
I talked to in Houston, Texas
two hundred of them in Houston
men who had been carpenters all their lives
and the white carpenters wouldn't let them in the union
and that meant they couldn't even work
on the Negro housing project
or on any kind of war building that was going on
and since there wasn't anything else left to work on
they were getting desperate. . .

There was a Negro welding class in Houston
just like the white classes
the whites got jobs welding in the shipyards
the day they finished their course
but the Negro welders
are working at common labor
or at nothing. . .

So it goes
all over the South
in munitions at Memphis
aircraft at Dallas and Nashville
at the Macon arsenal and Pascagoula shipyard
no skilled jobs for Negroes
and in many places
no unskilled ones either. . .
just whatever happens to be left over
when the white people are used up
or whatever work is too hot heavy or nasty
for white people to do
is what the Negroes get. . .
that's the way it still is
after eighty years

"Thenceforward and forever free"
were Lincoln's words
but he didn't stop there
no
he said more:
"and the Executive government of the United
        States,
including the military and naval authority thereof,
will recognize and maintain the freedom of such persons,
and will do no act or acts to repress such persons,
or any of them, in any efforts they may make for their
actual freedom."

Isn't it about time after eighty years
to make good on this
and to make good on
the Thirteenth Fourteenth and Fifteenth Amendments
to the Constitution of the United States?

I know there's a war on
but what is this war about anyway
how can we believe
how can the world's people believe
we mean to spread the light of freedom to the
        world's four corners
when there is such darkness
in America's own house?

Soon
it will be too late

## WHITE FOAM BREAKING

Hearing that he is dead
all I can think of
is the white foam breaking
over the spillway
and the lights in the hills

Who are these boys and girls reading by these lights
what lessons are they studying?

After forty years in the Congress of the United States
George Norris died simply a citizen
and in the Senate seat
which he had made more feared by the strong few
more loved by the weak many
than ever a Senate seat before
sat a small-town undertaker
destroying his work like a weevil in the good wheat

Nebraska
thanks for forty years of George Norris
who nourished the spirit of all this land
as your wheat the growing bodies of our children
How you must feel today
Nebraska
we know
who have also struck down blindly
the ones who loved us
and when it was too late
repented

Nebraska your treeless earth
spreads level to the sky's edge

your golden grain upturned to the sun and the blue
it's a long, long way from here
to Tennessee's hills
the rain-blackened cabins in the coves
the thin corn clinging to the slopes
the haggard children
the white water of the rushing streams

What is Tennessee to us?
you said
We want a man who will work for Nebraska
first last and all the time

George Norris grew too big for you
Nebraska
Your great plains bred a vision
vast as themselves and as bountiful

The hills and the plains are one earth
George Norris saw
and the people of both
one nation indivisible

Omaha Lincoln McCook and Grand Forks
the neighbor up the block
or beside the windmill whirling on the far horizon
are Nebraska you said
and when the Sheriff came to seize Jim's farm
you grabbed the pitchfork and went over

But when the people of Prague
of Warsaw Paris Athens Kharkov
wept in the streets as the hobnails rang on their cobbles
George Norris grabbed his pitchfork

Perhaps you understand him better
Nebraska
now that the neighbor up the block
or beside the windmill whirling on the far horizon
has a gold star in his parlor window

I intend to do as much as I can
George Norris said
the old man of 83
with the young heart
You tried to break it Nebraska
but it was too big for you
you were in it
but it had room for all the rest of us besides

He is gone
the simple citizen who marched at the head of us
but the march goes on
We march toward that America
which sleeps in the seeds he planted and others before him
as sure to grow
as wheat on Nebraska plains

He is dead
but the white foam breaks
over the spillway
and the lights in the hills
come on

# THEIR BLOOD CRIES OUT

I

Loving that part of the wide earth he was born on
though it was white man's country and he black
each year he laid by a few dollars
from his sharecrop half of the cotton
he and his family eating light to do it
going ragged and barefoot even in the wintertime
till he got his own piece of this earth
bought from the county for back taxes
and they wrote his name down as owner
there on the big book in the Court House
at Liberty (meaning freedom)
Amite (meaning friendship) County
Mississippi

The white men who had owned the land
but hadn't paid the taxes
came after him then with bullwhips
to teach him this was white man's country
and when the three of them had worn themselves out
stripping the meat from his back
he was still not dead and they figured he might talk
so they cut his tongue out with a switchblade

He died
and his blood soaked into the earth he was born on
the earth he had bought with his toil
and with his children's hunger

## II

Loving that reach of the wide sea he was born on
though it was white man's ocean and he black
he sailed it from a boy
fighting the rigging on the old four-masters
heaving coal down below on the freighters
standing watch at the wheel on the icy nights
while the years passed
and when the skipper cursed him for his color
or shipmates wouldn't share his foc'sle for it
he set his teeth and said nothing
but saved every scrap of writing
that proved he'd shipped AB or fireman
and every nickel of his pay
for his folks ashore

One war he sailed through
and they never got him
though he was nine days in a lifeboat
and when the next war came
he was about ready to quit
having the house all paid for
and something put by to live on
but he was needed

It was dusk when the planes struck
and he was at the wheel
he just slumped and that was all
until next day his corpse sewn in canvas
slid out from under the starry flag
into the wide sea he was born on

III

You ask me
what would I do if I were a Negro?
and I keep thinking of these two
who died
one on land and one at sea
murdered

If I were a Negro
I would swear the same oath I am swearing now
to avenge these men
and all the men like them and the women and children
white black yellow and brown
whose blood cries out for vengeance
all over the world

Being a Negro would change nothing
the same men would be my brothers
for brothers are not known by the color of their skins
but by what is in their hearts
backed up by their deeds
and by their lives
when it comes to that

# IV
## *1955-1959*

## AN AIR THAT KILLS

# THE IRON MAIDEN

Sometimes along palazzo corridors
or in the echoing vaults of castle keeps
or cold stone dungeons underneath the ground
among the torture wheels and windlasses
the thumbscrews and the monstrous metal boots
where molten lead was poured and out came foot
scoured whistle clean of flesh and tendon-strings
there you chance to see the iron maiden
black with antique rust and bloodcaked too
you fancy as you finger thrusting spikes

Demure and chaste her moulded face appears
the upright breasts declaring her a maiden
her supple figure draped in lines that cling
concealing nothing really worth revealing
save the hideous reality
couched within that hinged exterior
Once swung open and a man shoved in
manacled and gagged against his screams
the maiden clanged together and her spikes
gouged eyeballs out and speared his flesh all over

What a distance we have come from days
when barbarous implements like these were used
to enforce a uniformity of view
on those who doubted or were thought to doubt
the reigning imbecility of belief!
Now probes and oaths suffice to tame and curb
the unquiet questing spirit and should these fail
his relatives and friends will spy upon him
reporting all he says or thinks and last
the blacklist slowly buries him alive

## TO ALEXANDER MEIKLEJOHN
*On the Occasion of his Senate Testimony in Defense of Liberty*

I read your testimony and I thought
here is the man perfected that I knew
and reverenced next him who gave me life.
Too soon the long black limousine will stand
before your door and all unhearing you
will trundle off on casters while the winds
of elegiac oratory fill
the public prints and how the hearts will ache
of us who were your sons. Too late we'll carve
your stone. The time is now for rising up
and speaking out our love. Know then, dear man,
that mine has grown beyond the hero worship
of youth when your ideas broke the mould
of prejudice in which my mind was formed.
You let the world in on me, were the yeast
that set me boiling with desire to know
not merely but to do. I thought I loved
my country. You taught why America
deserved my love and all mankind's because
America was more than just a land;
it was the sum of all that men had won
against the ancient darkness. So believing
my life grew meaningful and where before
I felt myself an atom in the void
I now engaged to join with other men
to keep the light alive and specially
to oppose all those who in the name of light
would re-enthrone the darkness and betray
America. This they have nearly done.
And I myself in prime of life have felt
the anguished bitterness that exiles know

cut off and cast away. How easy now
to curse America, cast in one's lot
with enemies, back one usurping gang
against the other! But for you I think
I would have made this all-too-human error.
Despised, rejected as I felt the thought
of you restrained me at the brink. "What would
he think? What would he do himself?" So clear
the answer always came. "Believe!" you said,
"Don't let them drive you to despair! Fight on!"

## SCREENED

Most mornings you will find him
perched on the ledge beside the library
where homeless men foregather in the sun
like hungry crows along a fence
waiting for what they know by now
will never come

Around noon he leaves his perch
and heads toward Saint Anthony's to stand
with hat in hand for stew and beans
and afterwards he takes his daily walk
down the Embarcadero where
the ships are berthed

His destination is the tower
on Telegraph Hill and there he sits
all afternoon upon the parapet
watching the movement in the harbor
oblivious to the tourists
who stare at him

Among the gleaming cars the cameras
the sport togs and the jewelry
of elegant women he strikes a jarring note
in frayed and slept-in clothes
and people wonder why the police
don't move him on

It is a wonder that they don't
Perhaps they know how useless it would be
for by tomorrow they'd see him there again
or it may even be they still remember
what those pins on his lapel
were given for

Three torpedoes made of silver
meaning this man abandoned ship
that many times when wolf-packs roamed the sea
Some shipmates drowned some fried in oil
while some cracked up beside him
in the lifeboat

This man survived three sinkings
His grateful country then awarded him
three small torpedo pins for his lapel
and when the war was over
reviewed his seaman's papers secretly
and put him on the beach

Informants who for reasons of security
must remain anonymous avouched
that subject was suspected of subversive
leanings by his captain on one voyage
and was reported to have said he'd like
to visit Russia

Subject also was alleged
to have been prematurely anti-fascist
It was believed he'd had a hand one time
in hauling down the Nazi swastika
flying from a ship in port for which
police had clubbed him

And so the gold braid screened him off the ships
He asked to hear the charges and was told
the charges were a secret but if he
could guess them and reply thereto
his affidavit would receive
consideration

Thirty years at sea were thus
without redress or legal process ended
and since the man possessed no property
or trade beside the skill of seamanship
he became the public pauper
whom we observe

He sits upon the parapet
and follows with his eyes a ship
long gray and fleet that through the Golden Gate
makes way toward the open sea
The sunset burnishes the silver pins
on his lapel

## THE BETTER SORT OF PEOPLE

Our Negroes here are satisfied
They don't complain about a thing
except the weather maybe
whenever it's too cold to fish
for cat along the riverbank
But when they get away from here
up to Chicago or Detroit
and stay a while and then come back with notions
about the right to vote
or going to school with white folks
we sometimes have to get it through their heads
who runs this country
They're better off down here
or else why don't they stay up yonder?
A lot of them keep coming back
but somehow they've been spoiled
and need the fear of God
thrown into them again
Mind you I'm against the kind of thing
the ignorant rednecks do
I think it was unnecessary
to beat that little Negro boy to death
and throw his body in the Tallahatchie
He was uppity
no doubt about it
and whistled at a white woman
He probably learned that in Chicago
so we ought to make allowances
A good horsewhipping should have been enough
to put him back into his place
and been sufficient warning to him that
if ever he got fresh again

he wouldn't live to see Chicago
Those rednecks that abducted him
I doubt if even they
really meant to kill him when they started
working on him
They just got too enthusiastic
Like I say the better sort of people
down here in Mississippi
we love our Negroes
We wouldn't harm them for the world
This violence you hear so much about
is all the fault of low-down rednecks
poor white trash


CLIMATE OF FEAR

She was so emotional about it
I tried to tell her but she wouldn't listen
she ought to take these things in stride
and not get bothered
but you know how she was about the oath
That's all she talked about for months
and how when she got her credential
she'd make her living picking apples
before she'd sign the oath and teach
She told me once that she had joined
some group or other and when she found
it wasn't democratic she got out
and then it turned up on a list
That's why she carried on about the oath
She was afraid to sign
but all the same she did
That was just talk about the apples

She signed the oath and got a job
teaching in a little country school
and then one day she turned up here
frothing at the mouth
They were after her she said
Who? I asked her
Some parent in her school
had denounced her to the Board
because she talked about the Bill of Rights
in class one day and said that she believed
we didn't have the freedom we used to have
The Board was mostly ranchers
who've been fighting with the union up there
You probably read about them beating up
that organizer with a chain
They thought she must have meant them
so they got hot and called the FBI
Some agent from the city came and quizzed her
about her associations and so forth
He knew all about this thing
she once belonged to
and he kept asking her for names
but she refused to give him any
She was so frightened she was shaking still
She told me she was positive
she'd lose her job and then be prosecuted
because she'd signed the oath and in the end
she'd go to jail for perjury
I told her she was overwrought
and just imagining all that
I said let's go take in a show
but she rushed off again
Next thing I heard they'd found her car
parked by the bridge

## AN AIR THAT KILLS

Times were worse then
Jobs were hard to get
People were suffering more
but do you know
a man could breathe

It's as if the oxygen
were all exhausted
from the atmosphere
That's how I feel
and why I quit

Same land same sky same sea
same trees and mountains
I painted then
I guess the light went out
I saw them by

Don't make politics
out of what I say
It's just that something isn't here
that used to be
and kept us going

## REFLECTIONS OF A MAN WHO ONCE
## STOOD UP FOR FREEDOM

I'd say that gesture cost enough
but who can reckon up these things?
I'll hardly live to see the day
when I'll be justified at last
if ever that day comes. I wonder
often whether this is not
the onset of an age of darkness
covering all the earth. Could we
be quarantined against a plague
which saturates the atmosphere
we breathe and must continue breathing?
The world is indivisible
and so is freedom. Force and fraud
employed to scuttle human rights
in Spain or China, Mississippi
or Morocco, surely do
reverberate around the world.
They make the climate of our time
as certainly as when a storm
engendered in Siberia
with drifted snow can paralyze
New York and blast the orange crop
in Florida. Well, you might say
that it was my supreme misfortune
to recognize what kind of storm
was bearing down upon us. I sought
to warn the rest of you, for which
no thanks to me. The Jeremiah
role is rarely popular.
And so I got the old heave-ho
from my profession as perhaps

I should have known and after that
I found myself an outcast. Friends
quite naturally avoided me
lest my unclean touch defile them
and when I tried to find a job
all doors were closed against me. "Why,
it would be easier to place
a convict on parole than you!"
they told me at the office where
I went to seek employment. Then
my son quit college and my daughter
also. She'd wanted to be a teacher
like me. She's now a secretary
while my son, embittered, drifts
from job to job. Their mother failed
to appreciate my heroism.
Quixotic was the kindest term
she found for my behavior. First
we separated. After that
divorce was natural. We'd been
so close for more than twenty years!
She couldn't understand of course
and, do you know, sometimes I can't.
I really don't know why I threw
my life away for principle.
It seems an empty thing from here
shoveling behind these cows.

# THE SEARCH FOR TRUTH

Do I have freedom here
to search for truth and teach it to my students
the way I used to
before the oath and all these things came in?
Freedom is such a nebulous word
I don't know what you mean exactly
You'd have to define your terms
I teach the way I always have
but you know how it is
one goes on learning
one grows more experienced
one's taste becomes more disciplined
one realizes that the young
are prone to take things literally
and so a gradual approach to truth
is sometimes indicated
It seems to me a choice of values
is involved in this whole question
of so-called academic freedom
The public hires us to teach the young
Well and good
Would it then be fair for us
to betray the public trust
and teach our students what the public
does not approve of?
Clearly not and furthermore
we are dependent on the public
for our support
At last our salaries begin to match
those of professionals in other fields
and should we jeopardize these gains
with ill-conceived quixotic claims

to be a law unto ourselves?
Each year the legislature votes for us
another three per cent increase in pay
and look around you at these buildings
our new gymnasium our stadium
These mean we have the public's confidence
I wouldn't want to see this sacrificed
I don't think you would either
My attitude about the Mitchell case?
My opinion is that Dr. Mitchell
for all his undoubted brilliance
is not a man of tact and showed less judgment
than a full professor should possess
The police force as we know is far from honest
riddled with corruption if you please
What city's force is any better?
But to send one's students over town
sticking their noses into everything
with questionnaires
not even leaving out the brothels!
This was too much
He put the institution and his colleagues
to use a vulgar term upon the spot
with that investigation of the links
between police and prostitutes
That kind of thing is not our business
We should concern ourselves
with the eternal verities
and not the ephemeral passing show
We see events in true perspective only
generations after they occur
and all this hue and cry
over academic freedom
will surely seem a tempest in a teapot

131   *An Air That Kills*

a century or two from now
Of course it is a shame that Dr. Mitchell
had to go
He'd published many books
and was a credit to the faculty
May you quote me?
Oh no indeed!
I meant no criticism by my remark
It was a wise decision to dismiss him
I just meant. . .
Really I didn't mean a thing
but Mitchell was my friend
Don't quote me though
I want that off the record


ALTER CHRISTUS

Yes I remember him
a truly saintly priest
*alter Christus*
that is to say *another Christ*
such as we priests are all supposed to be
but yet you know a man like that
can do more mischief than a hundred
of the humdrum usual kind
That trouble he got into
could so easily have been avoided
Foolhardy was the word for him
I remember how for years he set his face

against all plans of his parishioners
to provide him with a car and driver
The Twelve Disciples went on foot he said
so trolleys should be good enough for him
Off he'd go to nowhere on the trolley
all alone and in the dead of night
taking the sacraments to some poor soul
regardless of the danger that he ran
The Ku Klux Klan was capable
of luring him to some abode of vice
on a fake call
and compromising him in people's eyes
thus doing all us priests an injury
The Bishop tried to make him see
the folly of his ways but he
just shook his head and smiled angelically
No harm could come to him he said
on such a holy errand
Our Lord Himself was there to guard him
How innocently trusting he could be!
So when this woman came to him and said
she'd like him to instruct her in the faith
he went ahead despite her character
Why she was a fallen woman
a very Magdalen!
He should have been more prudent
but no he treated her as if she'd been
a bona fide convert
and found a husband for her in the Church
Some kind of foreigner
I never went along with those who claimed
the foreigner had Negro blood
though to be sure his skin was rather swarthy
but still the woman's father had good cause

to feel aggrieved
He was a Klansman
a sort of jackleg preacher
who hung around the court house
and eked a living out by marrying couples
hot off the license bureau
Perhaps he felt his business was infringed
Right in broad day he took his gun
The priest was sitting on his porch
reading his breviary for Passion Week
and hearing feet come up the steps
he must have raised his eyes
and looked into the pistol's mouth
Some might consider him a martyr
but do you know
he actually did us all a lot of harm
The murderer was acquitted of his crime
by a jury packed with Klansmen
and the woman didn't even stick
She fell away soon afterwards
They always do that kind
The town believed that there had been
something between the two of them
The whisper went around
and where a priest's involved
such whispers find a ready ear
That's why I always say
we can't be too suspicious
of those who come to us
from lives of public vice and sin
with tears of feigned repentance
The safest thing for us to do
is shut our door against such persons
lest scandal enter in

# JUST PEANUTS

Down in Georgia
one of the 13
original States of the Union
near the town of Americus
named after the man
America is named for
there is a farm
called Koinonia
meaning "community"

This Koinonia farm
has belonged to the people who work it
for 15 years
They have built it up
from just about nothing
until it can support
all 60 of them
Sixty people on 1,000 acres
which is pretty good going
if you know Georgia

These people are all religious
calling themselves Christians
like their neighbors
and some of them are even preachers
but because they took Negroes in
and treated them as brothers
their Christian neighbors
got some dynamite

With this dynamite
these Christian neighbors of theirs

white citizens of Americus
real 100 per cent Americans that is
blew up a lot of Koinonia's property
Then their Christian neighbors
shot into houses at night
where people were asleep
sprayed the kids' play yard
with machine gun bullets
cut fences and let the hogs out into the road
even shot a few hogs to teach them better

Mostly though
their Christian neighbors
worked it strictly legal
All insurance on the farm
was cancelled out
Nobody would buy
the stuff produced at Koinonia
the milk soured
the eggs went bad
5,000 good hens had to be trucked away
and sold for culls

You would think the people of Koinonia
would quit and all go away
but they haven't
and they don't
They work all day
stand watches all night
pray for their Christian neighbors
and all that really bothers them
is where to get seed peanuts
to plant their fields

They sent two women out and a little boy
aged nine
to try to buy peanuts up and down Georgia
One place a man cursed these women out
for "dirty niggerloving whores"
and yelled to raise a mob
but they escaped with their little boy
aged nine
and went on to another town
but when night came and they drove back home
they still had found no peanuts

A few ton of peanuts
is all they need
just peanuts. . .


THE HONEY WAGON MAN

"Gre't God! Yond' come de honey wagon man!"
You scented him and then he hove in sight
perched on his tank, a turkey buzzard on
a carcass. "Whoa!" he'd tell his whip-scarred mule,
hop off, unhook his buckets, head for a row
of privies and dig in. The bucketfuls
would slosh. Then back he'd climb. You'd hear his whip
whistle and crack until that half-dead mule
would pull. I used to wonder to myself
where does he go at night when kerosene
glints through the chinks of shot-gun alley shacks
and families sit down to supper? Who
would run to hug his spattered legs? What woman
fix him some greens with fatback and a pone?

# INQUEST

A man lies dead today who yesterday
was working in his laboratory. He killed
himself. Killing himself he killed far more
besides. His research centered on the link
between twin scourges of mankind, cancer
and schizophrenia. This died with him.
Who knows what else? And all for what good end?
The man lies dead and cannot be subpoenaed
even by the Committee but awaits
that judgment which the Congressmen themselves
will some day stand to. He was accused of what?
Of nothing. If you prefer, of everything
that wild surmise can dream or sickest mind
invent. No fire in all the smoke? This much
perhaps, that in his youth he was deceived
by some who promised to redress world wrong.
(The Constitution left him free to make
his own mistakes.) Now, deep in a career
of dedicated service to mankind
he must confess, recant his early errors,
inform on friends whose guilt was no more real
than was his own. Or he must choose the way
of silence while men break him on the wheel
of public degradation, his sweating face
on television screens across the land,
a super-pillory where all may mock
and spit at him, his wife and children shamed
in every circle where they move, and then
the ultimate: his scientific work
halted, himself without a job or hope
of finding one, his family destitute. . .
And so he took the poison. What would you
have had him do, gentlemen of the Committee?

# THE SHORE OF PEACE

War called you from the mill
whence come those powerful hands and frame
that make men fear you when you wish
the measured gait as if you balanced
heavy beams upon your shoulders
and roughened face
like iron cast in sand

You drove a tank
in all that clanking troop
that rolled a storm of dust
across Tunisia's desert hills
toward the shore where Carthage stood
before the Romans rooted out
that rival city
and salted down the ground
lest dragon's teeth once more
should spring up there

A score of centuries
and who could count the wars
since chariot wheels of Scipio Africanus
dug ruts where now your whirling tracks
churned through the alkali
but when you reached the narrow pass
foes broke from ambush and with fire
of mobile guns blasted your column
The medics found you crushed
and burned beside your gutted tank
But not so crushed nor yet so burned
that you were privileged to die
Your native strength and all the arts

whereby we drag men back from death
so they may live to kill again
these saved you and restored you

That shore you then assaulted
where once the youth of Athens came
wading from their galleys through the surf
They were the lucky ones who died
beneath the Syracusan swords
The rest wore chains and quarried stone
until the alien sun
bleached out their graveless bones

Life-jacketed you stood on deck
in the lee of that hostile coast
when sudden wings screamed down
and LST joined Greek trireme
below
Among the bodies washed ashore
was yours
but once again
your pulse kept shuddering on

And once again
the surgeons sutured and trepanned
with rubber-fingered skill
until they could pronounce you fit
for bloody work
and such you did along a road to Rome
that barefoot pilgrims used to walk

You helped obliterate
that hallowed abbey on its crag
the motherhouse of all the west

where Benedict himself had walked
in meditation on his Holy Rule
but our guns in blasphemous choir
chanted the hour of compline there
and *Consummatum est* was heard once more
beneath a blackened sky

From Germany laid waste
victorious you sailed for home
Home was the same but you were not
The vacant talk of friends
the well-filled envelope of weekly cash
the soothing flesh of women
none of these assuaged
the deep hurt in you
that for all their scopes and rays
the doctors could not diagnose

You found asylum then
where Wasatch peaks at evening
throw shadows on the fields of hay
You moved among the silent brothers
robed and cowled in coarsest brown
about your tasks in scullery and barn
as Benedict had bidden

Straw upon a board your bed
your fare but bread and barley water
with green stuff from the garden
Long before the dawn you rose
and after lauds and matins sung
fasting still you labored
while stars yet shone
with all the luster of the Utah night

A year this was your world entire
a universe removed from men
and men's concerns for self
In all that while you spoke no word
save to confess your faults
Milking cows or dunging fields
your every act was prayer as deep
as psalms the choir monks chanted
within their carven stalls

What made you lay aside
your hooded Trappist habit?
What fiery-sworded angel
or was it conscience that forbade
you any longer to inhabit
this austere paradise?

You chose to make your home
with those who have no homes
the castaways of modern life
who in the roaring city are more lone
that hermits in their fastnesses
Immured are these each in his private hell
as on the flames they pour
the fuel alcohol and burn
themselves to deathlike sleep and wake
to pour and burn and die afresh

These sodden men
these women all degraded
you feed
as they file by with hanging heads
Each day you make the rounds
and beg on their behalf

stale loaves
fishes that stink
whatever men can't sell

From that same dish
whereon the wretched feed
you dine
That flophouse where they lay
their drunken heads each night
is also your hotel
Within your lumpy bed
you even share their bugs

And when one stifling afternoon
outside the Silver Dollar Bar
Willie the Weeper flips his lid
and shouts upon his knees
for God to strike him dead
while all his reeling cohorts circle
jeering round him on the sidewalk
you are the one who shoulders through the ring
to lift poor Willie up
and bear him tenderly away

# THE POLISHED CROSS

Inside the flawless chapel
for which the architect received a prize
Christ in low relief on granite
falls under a polished cross

Above the portal Mary mothers
a childish cluster while across
the terraced lawn within the offices
all gleaming glass the staff is gathered

"Embarassing our topic for today
but we must squarely face it
The sin of sodomy is rife among
our boys and drastic measures are required

Above all vigilance. . . a constant watch
Make sure by peering underneath the door
two boys are never found to occupy
 one toilet. . . Keep an eye upon the showers

Patrol the ballfield lest they hide
behind the backstop. . . Sneak beside the gym
and come upon them by the fire door
where weeds grow high and thick

Don't let a single pair of boys
get out of sight an instant
The kind we have here are abnormal
incorrigibly vicious

Let no new counselor imagine
he can accomplish anything

with kindness for the boys will think
it is the mark of weakness

Such men quit soon we find
or else we have to let them go
These boys are future criminals
and all they understand is force

Before we leave the subject
you might take down these names
of boys we have some reason to believe
corrupt the others. . . first Gonzales. . .

You'll find these Mexicans are all
inclined that way. . . Don't trust them. . .
Jackson next. . . Most Negroes are alike. . .
Sex mad and if they can't get girls

They'll take what they can get. . .
Antonelli. . . Italians are hot-blooded. . .
Smathers O'Rourke and Jankovich. . .
Degenerate stock in these three cases. . . "

Within the flawless chapel
for which the architect received a prize
a rough-hewn granite Christ
is nailed upon a polished cross

# OBSERVATIONS ON A GUIDED TOUR

We landed at Boston
one of their oldest towns
rich in monuments of greatness
We were driven to Bunker Hill
visited Lexington and Concord
saw the homes of Emerson
Thoreau and Lowell
champions they told us
of free speech and kindred errors
Afterwards we went to pay respects
to His Eminence
who favored us with a brief address
of greeting to America
Affairs were well in hand he indicated
No book was sold or cinema was shown
without his chancery's approval
Tradition was a stubborn thing he said
and Boston had been the lair
of pernicious liberalism once
but this by slow degrees had given way
to authority and orthodoxy
The faithful have the votes he said
to keep such men in office
as We in Our wisdom designate
We thanked His Eminence for throwing light
on how democracy works in Boston
and went aboard a bus for Plymouth Rock

# THE MASTER OF YELLOW PLUM MOUNTAIN

The Master on the night wind scented death,
his own that sought him out. Within his cell
he sat serene awaiting the encounter
when hubbub arose from the scriptorium
shattering his contemplation of last things.
Contentious monks were sharpening a point
of doctrine. Such overweening disciples shamed
the master, he reflected, fanging the Way
of Truth with tigerish disputes. He could
foresee the tonsured brawlers around his bier
all snatching for his robe, the sacred garment
that Bodhi-Dharma wore from India
when he brought first the Buddha's luminous words
across Himalayas to the Middle Realm.
Foreknowledge made the Master flinch. He should
now pass the robe to whom he chose, as once
he had been vested by his predecessor
of blessed memory. But which of these
proud meretricious monks would not debase it?
In his extremity he thought of one
new to the brotherhood, scion of men
who, yoked with crusted buckets, at back doors
begged excrement of close-stools which they hawked
to peasants for enriching garden plots.
For all his forebears' noisome trade, the gate
was opened to this man, the monastery
being short of kitchen hands. The most abject
of scullions now he pounded husks from rice
to fatten nobler bellies than his own.
The Master rang and had him fetched. "Leave us!"
The startled messenger withdrew at this
command. The dying Master slowly rose,

removing from his back the Dharma robe
and spread it over deep-bowed, trembling shoulders.
"Go, lest your holy brethren and their knives
discover your investiture. Avoid
the roads and seek the mountain fastnesses.
Your heart will know the day you must return
to men and teach." That night the Master died.
Missing the robe, the enraged community
in arms sought to apprehend the fugitive
but he had vanished in the highest snows.


## THE SIXTH GREAT PATRIARCH DECLINES

His crabbed brush indites: "Dread Lord! Your scroll's
superb calligraphy dazzles my eyes,
the eloquence of your minister my ears.
With tongue more silken than his gown
he bids me quit these rocky slopes for your
imperial palace. Could such inducements sway
my mind you'd gain another clown at court.
Your majesty mistakes his man. My bag
contains no magic tricks, no paper snakes
to affright the people or to make them clap.
The sutras are my only store, from them
I draw my poor powers, this robe the badge
of my superior emptiness. Husker
of rice was I. The Master for a sign
clothed me, the least of men, with Dharma. You,
I hear, are prone to heap old ivories,
patinaed bronze, pomegranite girls, eunuchs,
gold trinkets, jade, translucent porcelain

Would you augment your hoard with my person,
another on the random list of self-
indulgences, a man clothed in the robe
once worn by Bodhi-Dharma, sealed thereby
both saint and sage, the wonder of the time?
Must I for strings of cash augur tea-cups,
discourse of voices heard upon the mountains,
pose mystical conundrums for myself
to crack like lichee nuts? Most august sire!
I must decline to be your holy fool.
Foolish I am in truth but keep my house
amongst my thousand monks where it is hid.
Besides the Dharma on my back wears thin
and ragged. In pity of my nakedness
the beggars at your gate might toss me coins."


FATAL AUTUMN

Sun on the leaves of my orchard
makes fiery flakes and coins of gold
Firs and redwoods raise vast green walls
to a sky more blue than sea
The air is still as that first instant
after death
No whisper of a breath shakes any leaf
and the valley at my feet
might be a landscape of lost Eden
seen through tears

# DAY OF STRANGE GODS

The gale-whipped grass lies flat along the dunes.
Pacific combers flash and boil in sun.
Here in their time an elder vatic breed,
"Inquiring, tireless, seeking what is yet unfound,"
came questioning the surf. Motels pre-empt
the shore now. Rocks, the habitat of seals,
are spied upon by tourists who let fall
from airborne gondolas their popcorn bags.
Along the lethal beachside freeway speed
the uncouth behemoths of the Baalish cult.
Four-eyed they glare and flaunt proctitic rumps
more hideous than the mandrill's. Frost was here
and Whitman too, beard streaming in the sea-wind:
"But where is what I started for so long ago,
And why is it yet unfound?" The poet Whitman
although a prophet profited but little
from the divining trade. A backward farmer,
Frost pitched his hay himself, dispensing with
the blessings of machinery. Tonight
at 8:04, astronomers predict,
the satellite will re-appear, its arc
describing a trajectory fifteen
degrees above the crescent moon. "An age
of dark intent" the cryptic bard foretold
as he stood here in storm and hearkened to
the breakers' thunderous apocalypse.

# V
## *1961-1965*

## WOKE UP
## THIS MORNING

ONE MORE RIVER TO CROSS
*For John L. Salter, Jr.*

"The passage of the Patowmac through the Blue Ridge"
wrote the author of the Declaration of Independence
"is one of the most stupendous scenes in nature"
In the midst of this stupendous scene
on the second day of December 1859
the sovereign state of Virginia
hanged old Osawatomie Brown
(strange confluence of rivers)
for holding certain truths to be self-evident
which had been first enunciated
by the greatest Virginian of them all
A bystander at the hanging
one Thomas J Jackson
was struck by the incongruity of Brown's
"white socks and slippers of predominating red"
beneath sober black garb more appropriate to the occasion
A frivolous touch that "predominating red"
or could it have been a portent
Thomas J soon-to-be-dubbed "Stonewall" Jackson?
"Across the river and into the trees" you babbled
only four years later
while your blood ebbed away
ironically shot by one of your own
But it is still the second of December 1859
and you glowing with the vigor of a man in his prime
are watching while the body of Brown swings slowly
to and fro
in a cold wind off the mountains
for exactly 37 minutes before it is cut down
In less than half so many months
Thomas J Jackson

this stupendous scene plus 24,000 contiguous square miles
will no longer be Virginia
Its blue-uniformed sons will be ranged against you
in the Army of the Potomac singing
"John Brown's body lies a-mouldering in the grave
but his soul goes marching on"

Now you my friend
so akin in spirit to the earlier John
I have been seeing your picture in the papers
your head anointed with mustard and ketchup
at the lunch-counter sit-in
hoodlums rubbing salt in the cuts where they slugged you
or the police flailing you with clubs
blood sopping your shirt
but pure downright peace on your face
making a new kind of history
Now the people Harper's Weekly called
"this good-humored good-for-nothing half monkey race"
when John Brown sought to lead them out of bondage
are leading us toward that America
Thomas Jefferson foresaw and Abraham Lincoln
who once again sprawls dying in his theatre box
(Why must we always kill our best?)
The dastard in the bushes spots the crossed hairs
squeezes the trigger and Medgar Evers pitches
forward on his face while the assassin scuttles
into the night his beady rat's eyes seeking where to hide
his incriminating weapon with the telescopic sight
He heaves it into the tangled honeysuckle
and vanishes into the magnolia darkness
"God Sees the Truth But Waits"
The sickness is loosed now into the whole body politic
the infection spreading from South to North and West

"States Rights" "Freedom of Choice" "Liberty of the
    Individual"
Trojan horse phrases with armed enemies within
In the name of rights they would destroy all rights
put freedom to death on the pretext of saving it
Under the cover of Jeffersonian verbiage
these men move to destroy the Constitution
they feign to uphold
but their plots will miscarry
Who knows but that some unpainted shack in the Delta
may house one destined to lead us the next great step of
    the way
From the Osawatomie to the "Patowmac"
the Alabama Tombigbee Big Black Tallahatchie and Pearl
and down to the Mississippi levee in Plaquemines Parish
it's a long road
better than a hundred years in traveling
and now the Potomac again. . .
    *Summer, 1963*

## DON GREGORIO FROM OMAHA

Their constitution says we can't own land.
*Mordida* to officials, partnerships
with native stooges and you've got it made.
Greg Watkins picked an hacienda up
dirt cheap. He made his peons call him "Don
Gregorio" and take sombreros off
when he rode by like some old *hacendado.*
Big Em was "Doña Manuela" to all
her barefoot servants. Jesus, what a deal!
Then that *ejido* trouble started. Reds,
Greg called them, squatted on his property,
claimed they were starving so they had a right
to plow his best horse pastures up for corn.
Greg's got to buy a greaseball general
to run the buggers off with bayonets.


## AZTEC FIGURINE

"Ray-*hee*-nah!"
                    *"Ya voy, señora!"*
                                        All day on
the double with her mop and pail, huaraches
tattooing tile, small Aztec figurine
with no more bust or hip-span than a *chica*
at first communion. Three Caesareans
to pry her babies out. Her man is down
with ulcers. Even when he works he drinks
his little money up and lives with some
*puta.* Regina's shanty's built from cans
and crates high up the *Montuoso.* That's

the *barrio* without a water tap
for fifteen thousand people. Trucks come in
and sell it by the liter. There's a queue
at every out-house. Most just use a pot
and throw it in the street. Planes bomb the place
with DDT. At six Regina locks
her children in and goes to work. It's dark
when she gets home. She lights a candle then
beneath two pictures on the wall, Our Lady
of Guadalupe and by her side Fidel.


GONE

If you're looking for him here you might
as well give up. I doubt if he'll be back.
That sermon on our Christian duty to
pay tax for bombs was more than even he
could take. Maybe he's gone to Tennessee.
You've heard of how those Negroes registered
to vote and how their landlords threw them off
their farms and how the Negroes pitched a camp
and called it Freedom City. That's the kind
of place you're apt to find him. Jailed maybe
for bringing food and blankets in like that
preacher McCrackin all the elders and
high priests are out to get. Might even be
he ran the block to Cuba. Can't stop him
once he makes up his mind to see things for
himself. Could be he's building them a school
or housing for the folks of the *bohios.*
That wouldn't be a trade he'd need to learn.

## ON ACQUIRING A CISTERCIAN BREVIARY
(*For Father M. Louis, O.C.S.O.*)

Long cloistered these old volumes that my hands
profane. Rubbed spines spell golden seasons. *Pax
intrantibus!* How many hidden men
dipped honeycomb from hence and Samson-thewed
robustly strove till sepulture beside
the abbey church! Each has his somber cross
of naked iron with laconic plaque,
*sacerdos* and *conversus* leveled quite,
Don James whose tassel was abbatical
and bearded Frater Hyacinth who baked.
And will they rise triumphantly in choir
all faults expunged? These rubricated leaves
were thumbed by novices who now lie here.
But flowery tropes the prophecy and pledge,
a travesty on truth which holds no hope
for them? If so, how came they to be strong,
these silent monks? May desert rocks fill men
with food or venom work their cure? Embrace
such paradox who can. These books I'll have.

## ZION CANYON: EVENING

Named for a man, the Virgin river wears
an accidental grace. Her trout-rife reaches
darkle in the shadowed lees of colossi
whose thews of rosy stone she carved in moods
subliminal during her Maenad past.
What Byzantine basilica for all
its glittering glooms and fluted chrysoprase
but shrinks to bauble-scale measured by this
obdurate ecstasy of soaring rock?
Dour Mormon farm folk, first of our breed, fell
down on their knees before these high altars
that take the sunset molten on their planes.
The canyon fills with darkness but the light
lingers over Zion like an aureole.


## THE CAMALDOLESE COME TO BIG SUR

White habited hermits pace fog that streams
landward at compline bell. The ambrosial coast
harbors flesh-eaters, a poet's evil dreams.
Their ordure smears the cliffs. Now Jeffers lies
earthfast save prayer of these ransom his ghost,
so avid of dark. Cowled fathers, exorcise
his doomed lovers. Asperse, blest hands, these great
headlands commanding sapphire plenitudes.
Where blood-stained phantoms neigh and ululate,
let seraphim deploy hushed multitudes.

# TO LIVE AND DIE IN DIXIE

### I

Our gang
laid for the kids from niggertown
We'd whoop from ambush chunking flints
and see pale soles
of black feet scampering
patched overalls and floursack pinafores
pigtails with little bows
flying on the breeze
More fun than birds
to chunk at
Birds
were too hard to hit

### II

Old Maggie's sweat would drip and sizzle
on that cast iron range she stoked
but she was grinding at the handle
of our great big ice cream freezer
that day she had her stroke
It put a damper on my mother's luncheon
All the ladies in their picture hats and organdies
hushed up until the ambulance took Maggie off
but soon I heard
their shrieks of laughter
like the bird-house at the zoo
while they spooned in
their fresh peach cream

III

Asparagus fresh from the garden
my dad insisted
went best on breakfast toast with melted butter
so Rob was on the job by six
He used to wake me whistling blues
and whistled them all day till plumb
black dark when he got off
Times Mother was away
he'd play piano for me
real barrelhouse
(I liked it better than our pianola classics)
and clog on the hardwood floor
Rob quit us once to paper houses on his own
but white men came at night and sloshed
paint all over his fresh-papered walls
took the spark plugs out of his Model T truck
poured sand into the cylinders
then screwed the plugs back in
so when Rob cranked it up next day
he wrecked the motor
He came back to work for us
but I can't seem to remember
him whistling much again


IV

Black convicts in their stripes and shackles
were grading our schoolyard
At big recess we watched them eat
their greasy peas off tin
a tobacco-chewing white man over them
shotgun at the ready
and pistol slung
In class we'd hear them singing at their work

"Go Down Old Hannah"
"Jumpin Judy"
"Lead Me to the Rock"
I found a convict's filed off chain once in the woods
and took it home
and hid it


     V

Tired of waiting for Hallowe'en
Jack and I had one ahead of time
and went round soaping windows
and chunking clods of mud on people's porches
Mr. Holcomb though came out shooting
his 45
at us scrouged up against a terrace
across the street
He meant to kill us too
because his fourth shot hit betwixt us
not a foot to spare each way
so we didn't wait for him to empty the magazine
but just aired out a mile a minute
Next day
our mothers made us apologize
and Mr. Holcomb said he wouldn't have shot at us
except it was so dark
he took us for nigger boys


     VI

Confederate veterans came to town
for their convention
and tottered in parade
while Dixie played and everybody gave the rebel yell
but the Confederate burying ground near school
where the battle had been

nobody seemed to care about
It was a wilderness of weeds and brambles
with headstones broken and turned over
The big boys had a den in there
where they would drag the colored girls
that passed by on the path
and make them do
what they said all colored girls
liked doing
no matter how much
they fought back and screamed

### VII
The Fourth of July
was a holiday for everybody but people's cooks
Corinne was fixing us hot biscuit
when I marched into the kitchen
waving the Stars and Stripes
and ordered her to
"Salute this flag! It made you free!"
I just couldn't understand why Corinne
plumb wouldn't

### VIII
Old Major Suggs
ran for Public Safety Commissioner once
orating against the black menace
from his flag-draped touring car
and got just 67 votes
from a town that had 132,685 people in 1910
Things were well in hand back then
and folks were hard to panic
One night a chicken thief got into
old Major Suggs' hen-house

and made off with some of his Barred Rocks
The Major was slick
and figured out the path the thief was sure to take
back to niggertown
so he took a short cut through the woods
and hid behind a tree
The thief came staggering
beneath his sack of hens
and caught both barrels in his face
point-blank
"That nigger flopped and flopped"
old Major Suggs gloated long afterwards
"just like a big black rooster that you've axed"

IX

Spurgeon would daub designs on flowerpots
wheelbarrows
garbage cans
just anything he could get his hands on
though all he had was house-paint
and the kind of big flat brush
you slap it on with
My mother said
Spurgeon was what you call
a primitive
One Saturday evening
he was downtown window-shopping the pawnshops
gawking at all the jewelry
the pretty knives and pistols
when a mob came tearing round the corner
after another black man
but they made Spurgeon do

# FREE WORLD NOTES

### I
Lowdown white sonofabitch
comin in here and stirrin up our niggers to vote
lemme at him with this here blackjack
the cops done turned their backs

### II
I find you guilty Brenda Travis age 16
of an aggravatin breach of the public peace
for sittin down at the counter
of the bus station cafe
and I therefore sentence you
to one year's imprisonment
in the colored females' reformatory

### III
We the coroner's jury bein duly sworn
do find that State Rep'sentative Hurst
did whip Herbert Lee a nigra boy age 52
right smart over the head with the butt of his pistol
and did also fire a 45-caliber projectile
into the nigra's intercranial cavity
such bein the proximate cause of said Herbert's demise
and we do further find and pronounce
this act to have been justifiable homicide
the nigra boy havin provoked the Rep'sentative
unwarrantably
by insistin that he be registered on the book
and permitted to vote like a citizen

## "CHAINEY"

The field boss claimed his privilege. Her knife
quenched all his lust for black girls. She got life
in the Big Rock and swung a chain-gang pick
a quarter century before she broke.
To save her keep they kicked her out, paroled.
Root, hog, or die! Thereafter she despoiled
our garbage cans of what our pampered pets
repudiated. We capering white brats
dogged her around, mocking that tethered gait.
She shambled rolling-eyed down every street
in Birmingham, mumbling of "Jedgment." All
our minds were shackled by her chain and ball.

## THE CONVICT MINES
*Circa 1910*

"You sho' God bettah dig yo' task lessen
dat sweat-box git you or yo' bones be foun'
down some ole shaft." At dawn the shackled men,
lamps flaring on their caps, rode underground.
Four bits a day each convict brought on lease,
leading astute police to engineer
crap games to raid. Feeding just pone and peas,
mine owners heaped up fortunes year by year.
Murderers proved most reliable trusties
to stimulate output, wielding the thong
on shirkers and the sick alike. The fees
kept taxes down. Few deemed the system wrong,
it worked so well. Crime profited the state
and reinforced the black mortality rate.

## DIXIE BARD

The inexorable anapests of Dixie bard
Stella Foxhall DeRoulhac rode to rescue
white womanhood from brutish blacks. She charred
foiled rapists in slow fires as surely due.
Maternal cares oft frustrating her Muse,
Stella conveyed her daughter's custody
to a half-witted maid. The wench was loose
but never asked for Sundays off at three.
People, said Stella, were just pampering maids.
The half-wit in the bushes held Love's court
when school let out and soon the primary grades
practiced precociously the eldest sport.
Young Stella, barely six, showed future promise
of nymphomania, nor did prediction miss.


## MAN OF HONOR

His black barouche swept down the avenue
from his Ionic mansion's porte-cochere,
brisk hooves sounding matutinal tattoo.
Honeysuckle upon sequestered air
giving place to the aroma of pit privies,
he rode, scented silk handkerchief to nose,
by his abutting Negro properties
which squatted rump to rump in squalid rows.
Alighting at his bank's grave porticoes,
our subject laid aside *noblesse oblige*
during banking hours, though never would he foreclose
upon a social equal. Who'd then presage,
himself foreclosed in '29, his shame
would dictate that he sign in blood quit-claim?

# YOURS IN THE BONDS

Brother, your appeal's at hand. Our house
through long neglect decays. We must infuse
at once and massively the cash to heal
time's ravages, perpetuate the breed
we're noted for, oarsmen and athletes of
the bottle, clean-cut types whose fathers sit
on the Exchange. If we decline to act
the university will seize our house,
restore and lease it back to us at cost
of cherished principle. We might be forced
to take a Jew, Negro, or Indian.
Must we then foot the bill? A bitter choice!
Fat though our winnings from portfolios
and corporations we manipulate,
it's most repugnant to our principles
to make donations not deductible.
We joined our dearly beloved fraternity
to turn a profit, not incur a loss.
It was our lofty object to latch on
to lads who counted in the world, scions
of Munsingwear or Listerine or U.
S. Steel. The secret grip, the ritual
and all that garbage went along, quaint old
survivals from an age of squares who took
this jovial fraternal bit for real.
In 1853 Grandfather joined
at Williams, then a hick establishment.
The bumpkin "Prex" sat on a log and you
upon the other end and that, they claimed,
was education. Lots of good it did
Grandfather, all his wasted life a parson
who shared his pittance with the poor. When Father

matriculated at Cornell, Ezra's
egalitarian injunctions still
prevailed. A loutish school. The chapter house
was just a clapboard shack on Lake Street hill.
Later a turreted mansion was acquired
to accommodate a band increasingly
elite. In martial Teddy's times it burned
and boys were trapped. The brothers braved the flames
in vain attempts at rescue. They too died.
A note on White House stationery bears
high witness to their heroism. I
would not detract nor could I add a word.
Suffice it that the house burned down with loss
of life deplored by all. Insurance was
in force, the Lord be praised. Alumni dug
another bundle up and reared the pile
where I, a double legacy, was pledged,
initiated, taught to swill and wench.
Here I absorbed contempt for scholarship,
bitch goddess worship and a fake mythos
that made me dream myself superior
to all beyond the pale of our sweeping
greensward. Tricked out in coonskin coats and suits
from Brooks, we saw the world as our private
demesne to plunder rightfully while our
inferiors stood helplessly aside.
You ask me, brother, for my honest views.
My voice is for abandoning this relic
or willing it to the authorities to do
with as they wish. The brotherhood we preached
and practised was a fraud. Not love but hate
united us — the vilest kind that hates
a man because his name or skin is wrong,
oblivious to what at heart he is.

## SELF PORTRAIT IN A BAD LIGHT

My stripling authors flee the room to rub
congenial elbows in those dives where false
identities will pass. Cassocks withdraw
to contemplation of reforms. (But not
too radical nor yet too near the quick
of clerical privilege!) Dare I adjure
my Muse to plain of social wrongs in such
precarious circumstance? Must I be schooled,
veil plain speech in symbolic fog, costume
polemics for a merry morris dance,
practice new types of ambiguity,
and baffle those who sniff out heresy?
These shifts are common to the trade and steer
the prudent to snug haven when the gale's
a-starboard, blustery. No matter. The old
dog's teeth, to vary tropes, grow blunt. His eye
is blear. He shows more energy in dreams,
waggling his paws, than questing on all fours.
Who would heed his bark, grown querulous and faint?

## SILENT IN DARIEN

He glimpses through dividing wire gold thighs
and shameless buttocks of *señoras gringas*
at play like children on the grass, his hell
their paradise. Bloat-bellied, puny sex
exposed, his brood clamors about the shack
tin-cans and cartons built. Girls who survive
turn assets, spreading rachitic legs to ease
off-duty Yanqui personnel. His sons
besides the pimping trade will follow such
pursuits as untaught hands may ply for rice
and beans, fare foreordained, lucky those days
they feed. In crystal shrines across the fence
one sees prime cuts of beef — *por Dios!* — milk,
the precious nuggets of the hen enclosed
in cunning boxes, bins of liquors, sweets,
rare nutriments whose flavors, even names
are mysteries, done up in shimmering foil.
The sky goes black as when a hurricane
lowers from the Caribbean. Unobscured
the sun glows bloody red. There will be wind.

# UNDESIRABLES

*"I lift my lamp beside the golden door."*
    *Emma Lazarus. Inscription for the Statue of Liberty.*

The lifted lamp is guttering, near spent
its fuel. Double-barred the golden door
which, when it opens, opens on a chain.
Where throngs poured through, police interrogate
each refugee, admitting but the few
who pass security and kiss the Book.
Carl Schurz would be excluded with his staunch
compatriots of Eighteen Forty-Eight
whose rebel blood caused liberty to grow
in their adopted land. Could Juárez get
a visa from the State Department? Would
the FBI clear Dvorak, known to be
in sympathies an anti-monarchist?
(Deport the New World Symphony!) Martí,
the Cuban foe of imperialism? Lorca,
the anti-fascist poet? These men were all
subversive as in earlier times Tom Paine,
Pulaski, Lafayette. The authorities
would surely bar such undesirables.

## THE SEED OF FIRE
*For Highlander Folk School*

The celluloid is old. It snaps and must
be spliced. The worn-out sound-track garbles words.
But here they are, the marching union men,
the girls with banners. Pitiful! A torrent
of mountain water plunging from the rocks
to lose itself downstream in stagnant sloughs,
mud-clogged meanderings and stinking pools.
The nation rots. What we were once looks out
of this old film with shining eyes. Where did
we miss our way? New men rise up with skins
dark-hued to take the vanguard place of those
grown compromised and well content to rake
fat winnings from the gamble of death. Dark too
those women who indomitably face
plantation lords and teach sea-island folk,
disfranchised all their voiceless lives, to stand
and vote. Here is the continuity,
the precious seed of fire in these sad ashes.

A COMMEMORATIVE ODE

*For the 60th Anniversary of the Beecher Memorial*
*United Church of Christ in New Orleans*

Old church with the same name as my own
you and I were born in the same year
It has taken two generations to bring us together
Now here we are in New Orleans
meeting for the first time
I hope I can say the right thing
what the man you are named for
might have said on one of his better days
He was my great-great-uncle
but come to think of it
he was instrumental in my founding too
Rolled in a tube at home I have a certificate
signed by Henry Ward Beecher
after he had united my grandfather and grandmother
in the holy bonds of matrimony
at Plymouth Church in Brooklyn
The year was 1858
and James Buchanan was President
The South was riding high
making the North catch and send back its escaped Negroes
and it looked to most people
as if slavery were going to last forever
but not to Henry Ward Beecher
which I suppose is why you named your church for him
He certainly helped to change all that
together with his brother Edward and his sister
whose name was Harriet
and Mr. Lincoln and General Ulysses S. Grant
and a large number of young men
who wound up under the long rows of crosses

at Gettysburg Chickamauga Cold Harbor and such places

Nineteen hundred and four was a better year
than 1858
and the building of this church was a sign of it
It was no longer a crime to meet and worship by yourselves
with your own preacher
your own beautiful songs
with no grim-lipped regulators to stand guard over you
nobody breaking up your services with a bull-whip
Yes this was some better
Booker T. Washington was in his hey-day
the apostle of segregation
"We can be in all things social as separate as the fingers"
he said and Mr. Henry Grady the Atlanta editor
applauded him to the echo
as did all the other good white folks around
and they said
"This boy Booker has a head on his shoulders
even if it is a nappy one"
Dr. Washington was 48 years old at the time
but you know how southern whites talk
a man is a boy all his life if he's black
Dr. Washington was a pragmatist
and settled for what he could get
When they announced that dinner was served in the dining
    car
he ate his cindery biscuits out of a paper bag
and when George the porter made up berths in the Pullman
he sat up all night in the Jim Crow coach
Because of his eminently practical attitude
Dr. Washington was successful in shaking down
the big white philanthropists
like C. P. Huntington the railroad shark

or was it octopus
and Negro education was on its way

Old church
since 1904
you and I have seen some changes
slow at first
now picking up speed
I have just come from Mississippi
where I saw churches like this one
burned to the ground or smashed flat with bombs
almost like Germany when I was there in 1945
only these Negroes were not beaten people
They sang in the ashes and wreckage
such songs as *We Shall Overcome*
and *Let My Little Light Shine*
*O Freedom!* they sang
*Before I'll be a slave*
*I'll be buried in my grave*
*and go home to my Lord and be free*
They sang *I'm going to sit at the welcome table*
*I'm going to live in the Governor's mansion*
*one of these days*
I heard three mothers speak
who had made the President listen
and "almost cry, or he made like he was about to cry"
when they told him
how their homes had been dynamited
"It's not hard to be brave"
one of these mothers said
"but it's awful hard to be scared"
I expect to see her statue on a column in the square
in place of the Confederate soldier's
one of these days

Remember
slavery looked pretty permanent in 1858
when it had just five years to go
and now in 1964
the White Citizens' Councils and the Ku Klux Klan
think they can keep their kind of half-slave South forever
Their South isn't on the way out
It's already dead and gone
only they don't know it
They buried it themselves
in that earthwork dam near Philadelphia Mississippi
when they thought they were getting rid of the bodies


## IF I FORGET THEE, O BIRMINGHAM!

I.
Like Florence from your mountain.
Both cast your poets out
for speaking plain.
II.
You bowl your bombs down aisles
where black folk kneel
to pray for your blacker souls.
III.
Dog-torn children bled
A, B, O, AB as you.
Christ's blood not more red.
IV.
Burning my house to keep
them out, you sowed wind. Hear it blow!
Soon you reap.

# WOKE UP THIS MORNING WITH MY MIND SET ON FREEDOM

A flood of song
breaches the levee
swamps cabins in the cotton
sweeps Natchez-under-the-hill

The flock escapes old shepherds
who in the dust of the stampede
incredulous and dazed
lumber along out of breath

Frock coats and crinolines
built nothing here
but skilled black hands
reared all this beauty

Which one of these
white-colonnaded bastions of the ancient lie
among moss-oaks and magnolias
will be our Freedom House?
*Natchez during the demonstrations, September, 1965.*

# A HUMBLE PETITION TO THE PRESIDENT OF
   HARVARD

I am, sir, so to speak, "a Harvard man."
In legendary times I lugged my green
baize bag across the Yard to sit while fierce
Professor Kittredge paced his podium
in forkéd snowy beard and pearl-grey spats,
mingling his explications with his views
obscurantist on life and letters. Texts
prescribed for us were caponized. Prince Hamlet
made no unseemly quips anent the thighs
Ophelia spread for him nor did that poor
crazed beauty sing the naughty songs for which
she's celebrated. Nice young men were we
in Kitty's class. Extra-curricular
our smut—Old Howard queens of bump and grind,
the Wellesley girls who warmed our chambers. Such
the Harvard I recall: Widener's great hive,
whose honeyed lore we rifled and bore off
on index cards, all nutriment destroyed;
the home of Henry Wadsworth Longfellow;
dank mournful halls; an ill-proportioned pile
commemorating boys who'd marched away
to die for causes the professors had
endorsed, knowing infallibly which side
God and their butter were upon. Our boot-
legger was Polish. Christened Casimir
Zwijacz he'd changed his name to Lawrence Lowell
after fair Harvard's president. Ambushed
and shot by high-jackers who coveted
his rot-gut load, Lowell barrelled his truck
back from Cape Cod and, bandaged bloodily,
made punctual deliveries to all

his Cambridge clientele, fresh luster shed
upon an honored name. *Per aspera!*
Nostalgic reminiscences brought on
by your most recent bulletin. I learn
of your "Commitment to the Modern," penned
expressly for Old Grads by Lionel
Trilling, D. Litt., a masterpiece, I thought,
of academic prose, so clear and yet
so dark. It cheers me that you do not change
at Harvard, like *castrati* whose voices
retain their boyish purity. Trilling
delights me with his cadenced double-talk.
"The radical," says he, and dares to add
"subversive" in a breathless tone, is like
to be predominant among the forces of
our time. Already on the student mind
(so impatient of the rational) this force
works powerfully. Oppose it, counsels he,
in order that it may grow strong and strike
deep roots. "Bland tolerance," he trills, "subverts"
subversion, makes it wither on the vine.
The way to nurse dissent is to impose
conformity — the logic's Lionel's —
and carefully exclude dissenters from
the faculty. Would we aid William Blake
to mew his mighty youth? Deny stipends.
Give ninnies suck at Alma Mater's teats.
Wean Blake. Choose Doodle in his stead as Poet
in Residence lest William be suborned
by excess of ease and lick the arses that
require booting. The University
of Hard Knocks is the proper berth for such
obstreperous geniuses. "When we are scourged,
they kiss the rod, resigning to the Will

of God," as Swift observed of moralists
like Trilling. Fend from me, I beg you, sir,
offers of chairs magnates endow. Waylay
me with no teaching sinecure. (Degrees
sufficient to impress the Dean are mine.)
Summon me never to recite my verse
before a convocation in my honor
nor to appear in doctoral costume
as orator at Commencement. Such coddling,
as Trilling rightly says, would work my ruin.
Let me forever cope with penury
and cold neglect. Let me be ostracized
for practising ideals you fine folk
are given to prating of at ceremonies.
Do what you please with me defunct. Put up
a plaque. Dissect my corpse in seminars.
Transmogrify my bones to index cards.
Hang my dead portrait in the library
and crucify your living rebels still.

## FINISHING SCHOOL

A ten-foot fence that's topped with barbed wire strands
surrounds this finishing school. In star-marked cars
the girls are fetched by uniformed escorts.
Sad debutantes! Lovers you shall not lack.
Trapped female animals surpass the male
in viciousness. To frustrate vigilance
and woo each newcomer with arts practiced
on Sappho's isle is all their frenzy here.
The pool's a passion tank. About each pair
of furtive amorists fair mermaids sport
to screen their throes of love. Fine scenery
encompasses the school and visitors
exclaim. The picture windows when kicked out
by inmate heels make serviceable dirks,
stilettos, spears, from which psychologists
shrink back, and even deputies with guns.

## A DIXIE HERO

Ole Raymon seed this black boy comin long
the walk an didn' lahk his looks so he
retch down an grab a gre't big rock an stove
damn nigguh's head in faw him. Nevah seed
so comical a thang sence Ah been bawn.
Ole Raymon bust a hole big as a half
a dollah spang in his fo'head. Cain't kill
no nigguh thataway. They skulls is bone
clean th'oo. Well, Raymon got th'owed outa school.
Shit, not faw that. He cussed the principal.

# A MEDITATION ON THE FLAG
*1862-1962*

Framed in her attic window in Frederick town,
shaking her banner out at dour Stonewall,
 bidding him *Shoot, if you must, this old gray head,*
*But spare your country's flag,* Dame Barbara
gave Whittier his noblest theme. Her myth
enshrines a symbol sacred to us once
though worse defiled now than by rebel shot.
Green hills of Maryland wall Frederick
as then but chimneys dwarf the "clustered spires."
Old Glory floats above a devilish hive
where secretly we manufacture toxins
so potent that an ounce could wipe out millions.
Here traitor scientists impregnate hordes
of bugs with virulent bacteria
so each mosquito, fly, louse, tick, and flea
carries a war-head of bubonic plague,
typhus, the bloody flux, cholera, anthrax,
or yellow-jack. Here pathogens are bred
to blight the healthy crops and famish nations.
Here too in squat retorts, alembics, vats
they brew, distill and synthesize the fumes
to drive whole cities mad, strike children blind
and slay in paroxysmal agonies
windrows of innocents for others' deeds.
What crime in all man's ghastly history
can stand with this prepared in Frederick
beneath the poet's "symbol of light and law?"
Haul down the stars and stripes! Run up the flag
we really serve—black, with the skull and bones!

# WISDOM OF THE ABBOT MACARIUS I

Said he: "I can no longer sanction
    any war for any purpose
        under God's sun or stars"
And they put him in chains

Said he: "I can no longer sanction
    any war for any purpose
        under God's sun or stars"
And they showed him the scaffold

Said he: "I can no longer sanction
    any war for any purpose
        under God's sun or stars"
And they laid his head on the block

Said he: "I can no longer sanction
    any war for any purpose
        under God's sun or stars"
And the ax fell

Whereupon the multitude fell silent
    thinking
        well
He could be right

# BESTRIDE THE NARROW WORLD

*"Why, man, he doth bestride the narrow world*
*Like a Colossus, and we petty men*
*Walk under his huge legs and peep about*
*To find ourselves dishonourable graves."*
JULIUS CAESAR, I, ii.

We dangled them upon the edge a week
letting them savor death and then reprieved
them from their jeopardy a space. The style
is new. The abominations of his war
moved Lincoln to unmanly tears. Perhaps
he pondered Scripture overmuch. We too
bring God into our speeches. Fustian
we spout as well to cloak our naked sword
in words of righteous tone. Small matter if
the skeptical are unconvinced. We have
the countervailing force to make them cringe.
No power makes us stoop to parley. Proud
as pterodactyls in their prime are we,
mighty as mammoths whose unrivaled thews
the tundra binds in ice perpetual.

## CONFORMITY MEANS DEATH
*For Bertrand Russell*


Our time's true saint he is, whose fealty
transcends the bounds of nation, tribe and clan,
embracing all who inhabit earth and their
inheritors. The voice we hear is more
than his. Through him the unborn of our loins
plead that we interpose our bodies now
between them and the Juggernaut we've built.
"Conformity means death!" No rhetoric
but starkest truth he speaks. Throw road blocks up
to Armageddon with your flesh. Besiege
the supine parliaments which veto peace
and cast their purchased votes for war. Let them
not sleep for your outcry. Fast unto death
if need be. Nail your picket signs upon
the doors of churches that usurp the cross
and grossly mock the One they feign to serve.
(He is not mocked but bides His awful time.)
Then rise! "Protest alone gives hope of life!"

# A VETERAN'S DAY OF RECOLLECTION

We'd liberated Naples and the Wops
had come aboard to work cargo. This starving
Spick slipped a can of rations underneath
his lousy rags. We drilled him. At Marseilles
we mowed a stevedore down for pilfering
some Spam. The Battle of the Bulge was on,
V-bombs had knocked out Antwerp but the God
damned Frogs struck every ship of ours in port.
P-40's shot up Palermo for the hell
of it. Pinpoint objectives? Tenements!
Krauts wreched Le Havre's docks and blew. The town
was open. Flying Fortresses blasted
it flat and left some thirty thousand dead
allies of ours. Christ, how those ruins stank!
GI's in Germany went "one to shoot
and three to loot." We always gave
a Hershey to the frauleins that we ganged.

ENGAGEMENT AT THE SALT FORK

Like tumbleweeds before the wind we moved
across the continent's huge heedless face.
Fat sheriffs' radios kept hot with news
of our invasion. Squad-cars tailed the walk.
Blasts born on Yukon tundras knifed us through
and buffeted our sign: *Man Will End War*
*Or War Will End Man.* Handful that we were,
armed men patrolled us, secret agents sped
ahead to warn the elevator towns.
Christians heard now that if they harbored us
and let us spread our sleeping-bags on floors
of Sunday schools, religion would be lost.
Whoever opened up his door to us
was spotted by a telephoto lens,
proclaimed suspect, anathema to all
right-thinking patriots. As if we were
the ghosts of banished Cherokees come back,
the guilty Strip shook in its cowboy boots.
We camped one night beside the Salt Fork, near
a town through which they'd hustled us with guns
and imprecations lest ideas start
an epidemic there. Our campfire lit,
potatoes boiling and someone's guitar
strumming *Down by the Riverside,* people
began to drift in from the country round.
Skylarking students with a bugle, torches,
burlesquing us with signs: *Workers Arise!*
*You Have Nothing to Lose but Your Thirst! Drink Beer!*
Good kids they proved to be and soon knocked off
the clowning. Faces in the firelight grew
into hundreds, boys with their dates, big-hats
from nearby ranches, preachers whose wives had brought

us popcorn, apples. A dozen arguments
swirled into being as good-humoredly
they challenged us to win their minds with fact
and logic. Raw though the night, shirt-sleeved they stood
and battled with us till they came to see
the meaning of our walk. Some would have joined
had we sought that. One horse-breeder, Stetsoned
and powerful of frame, told of campaigns
he'd fought in Italy. Fondling his son,
a lad of eight, he blessed our walk for peace.
"Each war *we* fight, *they* promise is the last,"
he said, "and here they go ag'in. This boy
is one they ain't a-goin' to git, by God!"
Long after midnight it was when the last
of them went home. I could not sleep for pride
in these my people, still square-shooters, still
ready to tote fair with the other man.
I could not sleep for sadness too, to think
how these great hearts are gulled with lies.
God help the liars when my people wake!

JOHN BEECHER, although a great-great-nephew of Abolitionists Henry Ward Beecher and Harriet Beecher Stowe, was
brought up in Birmingham, Alabama, where his father was an
executive of U. S. Steel. From the age of 14 when he finished
high school, John Beecher worked in steel mills. Twelve-hour
shifts on the open hearth furnaces turned him into a rebel and a
poet.

He attended VMI, Cornell and the University of Alabama,
was a graduate student at Harvard and the University of
North Carolina, and traveled in Europe for a year. After teaching at Dartmouth and the University of Wisconsin, where he
was on the staff of Dr. Alexander Meiklejohn's famous Experi-
mental College, Beecher for eight years administered New Deal
programs in the South, dealing with the rural and urban poor,
migratory labor, and Negroes discriminated against in employment. Among his posts was that of regional director for President Roosevelt's original Fair Employment Practice Committee.

During World War II Beecher served aboard the racially
integrated Liberty ship, "Booker T. Washington," and wrote a
book, *All Brave Sailors,* which Earl Conrad called in the *Chicago
Defender,* "a milestone in literature and politics. . . the strongest
stuff to come out of the war."

Beecher was an editor in Washington, D.C. following the war
and later taught at San Francisco State College. Refusing to
sign the unconstitutional Levering Act oath adopted by the
State of California in 1950, he became a working rancher. He
and his wife founded a private press to print his poetry, win-
ning several awards.

In 1958 Beecher moved to Arizona, teaching at Arizona
State University. From 1963 to 1965 he was Poet in Residence at
the University of Santa Clara in California. During 1966-67 he
was Visiting Professor at Miles College, a Negro institution
in Birmingham. Most recently he has made field studies of
black power and poor white organizing movements in the
South as a special consultant to a private foundation.